Katya Buchleitner

Glimpses of Freedom

MASTERS OF PEACE

edited by the

UNESCO Chair for Peace Studies
of the University of Innsbruck / Austria

Volume 2

LIT

Katya Buchleitner

Glimpses of Freedom

The Art and Soul of Theatre of the Oppressed in Prison

LIT

Bibliographic information published by the Deutsche Nationalbibliothek
The Deutsche Nationalbibliothek lists this publication in the Deutsche Nationalbibliografie; detailed bibliographic data are available in the Internet at http://dnb.d-nb.de.

ISBN 978-3-643-50203-2

A catalogue record for this book is available from the British Library

Krotenthallergasse 10/8
A-1080 Wien
Tel. +43 (0) 1-409 56 61
Fax +43 (0) 1-409 56 97
e-Mail: wien@lit-verlag.at
http://www.lit-verlag.at

LIT VERLAG Dr. W. Hopf
Berlin 2010
Fresnostr. 2
D-48159 Münster
Tel. +49 (0) 2 51-620 320
Fax +49 (0) 2 51-922 60 99
e-Mail: lit@lit-verlag.de
http://www.lit-verlag.de

Distribution:
In Germany: LIT Verlag Fresnostr. 2, D-48159 Münster
Tel. +49 (0) 2 51-620 32 22, Fax +49 (0) 2 51-922 60 99, e-mail: vertrieb@lit-verlag.de

In Austria: Medienlogistik Pichler-ÖBZ, e-mail: mlo@medien-logistik.at

In Switzerland: B + M Buch- und Medienvertrieb, e-mail: order@buch-medien.ch

In the UK: Global Book Marketing, e-mail: mo@centralbooks.com

In North America by:

Transaction Publishers
New Brunswick (U.S.A.) and London (U.K.)

Transaction Publishers
Rutgers University
35 Berrue Circle
Piscataway, NJ 08854

Phone: +1 (732) 445 - 2280
Fax: + 1 (732) 445 - 3138
for orders (U. S. only):
toll free (888) 999 - 6778
e-mail: orders@transactionpub.com

And I say to you that not a single person is born in the world
who has not a certain capacity which will make him proud,
who is not pregnant with something to produce,
to give birth to something new and beautiful,
to make the existence richer.
There is not a single person who has come into the world empty.

Osho

TABLE OF CONTENT

PREFACE

I set out writing a Master Thesis in order to complete the MA Program for Peace Studies and International Conflict Transformation in Innsbruck, Austria. Eager to research, I delved into the topics of freedom, Theatre of the Oppressed and the application of Theatre of the Oppressed in prisons. The title of my MA Thesis had been: *Creating Sparks of Freedom in Prison - Theatre of the Oppressed as an "art of inspiring people to turn themselves inside out, transform their suffering into art, their art into awareness and their awareness into action."* This quote was taken from the homepage of Gabrielle Roth, the creator of the *5 Rhythms*. Apart from being an extraordinary dancer, artist and musician she has written three books that have been an important source of inspiration for me during my writing process. My writing process had somehow been carried by the *5 Rhythms*. They taught me that all aspects in life are perpetually changing and that we constantly move through the rhythms of flowing, staccato, chaos, lyrical and stillness. Thus this theory and practise supported me to jump and ride on life's rhythms in any form in which they showed up. I kept on writing – and dancing – in periods of confusion, chaos and clarity; in times of resolute determination, flowing relaxation or desperate stagnation; in phases of relieved celebration and introspective stillness. After more than a year of perseverance the last pages had been written, the Master thesis submitted and I received my diploma. Yet, the adventure did not finish at that point.

Soon, I received the offer to have my thesis published as a book. This meant to review it, to ask a native English speaker for her editing and to make all necessary changes before I would dare to present it to an international audience. Furthermore I requested eight close friends to give me their most straightforward and ruthless feedbacks. These friends who are my confidants, my muses as well as my most important, radical critics opened my eyes to facets that I missed, forgot or unsuccessfully ignored. Thus, this book is the result of research, discussions, philosophical questions, introspection – and friendship!

FOREWORD by Michael Balfour

All this useless beauty: prison theatre and some tales of the unexpected

In 1947 Cecil Collins, a British artist, wrote an introduction for a book of reproductions of his series of paintings and drawings, 'The Holy Fools'. Early on he quotes the French philosopher Jacques Maritain, who describes a growing unease with modernity, because it is based, as he sees it, on the unnatural principles of 'the finality of the useful' (Collins 1947, 1). Collins picks up on this and suggests:

> In a respectable practical society, where everybody is useful, the poetic imagination in man is an anachronism, an irritant that disturbs the chemical sleep of habits of such a society by making it conscious of the degradation of its mechanization.
>
> (Collins 1947, 3)

The intentions of artists in prisons often reflect the desire to use the arts to reawaken dormant emotions, to create 'fissures' (Katya uses the term in this book) where imagination can flow. Why artists are given the permission to do so by an institution more often geared toward punishment, or passive containment at the very least, is always a point of contention. Looking through the glass darkly it is possible to see that the arts can be used in the same way that drugs are 'allowed' to be in prison – it shuts the prisoners up for a short time, it distracts them and 'keeps them occupied'. The arts also can also provide a methodology for institutions to demonstrate their progressive approaches to rehabilitation. The arts can get co-opted into this disciplinary discourse, describing themselves as criminogenic interventions, and deliver drama techniques to dissect individuals.

By way of an example of this, I remember delivering a training course for prison officers to use a drama-based group work programme called Blagg! The prison 'specialised' in young offenders, and was in fact an old borstal that looked like it was a work house from the Victorian era. More modern blocks had been added on to cope with the growing prison population. The education staff considered it a success if they can get the 'lads' to call their girlfriends by their name, rather than a five letter word. The prison guards were sceptical – the training was a skive for them – and a chance to hijack another do-gooder. Despite everything and in spite of themselves, the guards got very involved with the training. At the end of the session, one of the guards sat back, and more to himself than anyone else, says 'this is a brilliant tool for finding out what's really going on in the heads of the little buggers'. Theatre as 'enhanced interrogation' within the panopticon?

The degradation inherent in 'useful' arts intersects worryingly with prison theatre's meta-rationale of purposeful social intervention. Jackson (2007, 28) notes how few writers on this form of 'applied' theatre seem directly concerned with the artistic dimension of the work. He picks up on a familiar, but relevant, debate about the tension between theatre's aesthetic elements and the utilitarian or instrumental work that has a 'job to do' (Somers 2006, viii). Similarly Schonmann's (2005, 32) analysis of the three main drama education conference programmes over the last ten years demonstrates that applied researchers are all too often governed by instrumental and practical concerns; and wonders if there is a 'tax' on aesthetic-artistic language in the discourse (35).

Katya's practice as described in this book seems remarkably free of such restrictions. Perhaps, as she questions herself, she is idealistic in her outlook. She uses the language of a romantic in terms of the need for sparks of freedom, and personal growth through the theatre, and clearly has a passion for social change and individual empowerment. The confidence of romantic convictions is important to maintain, particularly in an environment geared towards the opposite. You need to be eternally naïve, and forever critical to negotiate the complexities of the prison landscape.

Social change turns up in the most unexpected of places. One of the performances in my top ten list of beautiful moments of theatre is a monologue from a lifer in a high security prison in North of England in 1995. It was in a break during a week-long drama residency. It wasn't a particularly good project – the lads kept disappearing to nick things from a metal-making workshop next door. I was 15% drama facilitator and 85% junior prison guard. As the lads went off for 'canteen' an Asian boy, no more than 24, stayed back. We started chatting, he joked about my single lack of ability to keep 15 lads in one room at one time. I am not sure where it came from, because asking personal questions of a prisoner was an unspoken rule. But it came. At first fragmented, and then seamlessly paced. A beautiful life history, full of lies and honesty, tension and pathos. It was funny, tragic, heart-breaking and ironic – delivered with power and restraint. It lasted maybe 15 minutes, just enough time for him to finish and pause, before someone ran in with a hack-saw, and the moment was gone.

Was this a 'disruptive' moment of theatre? A spark of freedom? Not in conventional terms. Did it derive from the deep aesthetic engagement of the work? Probably not – we could have been basket weaving. Was it performance? For me absolutely. An accidental performance: incidental, informal and at the margins of any purpose and intention. Did it create change and transformation? Yes. It changed me profoundly.

Michael Balfour
Griffith University, Brisbane, Australia

My Perspective

My momentary Perspective

> "See, without this flame of discontentment, you will never have this drive, which is the beginning of creativity."[1]

On Thankfulness and Discontent

I grew up in Austria, a country which since I was born in 1985, has not seen wars, armed conflicts, famines or any other form of suffering that has struck the whole population – one might call it a *peaceful* country. My parents raised me lovingly and the majority of time in a patient and supportive way. My family's house is located in a secure and calm environment, a five-thousand inhabitant town, embedded in scenery of fertile acres and green meadows.

Gradually I discovered with gratitude that I had been born into a nourishing, strengthening environment which gave me every opportunity to make my own choices and grow in my own way. However, since my teenage years, precisely since my first stays abroad for half a year in Mexico and Thailand, a conflictive insight entered my life which has accompanied me from then on: The realization that my own world is simply a tiny fragment of the whole and that there is a lot of suffering, starvation, violence, oppression and injustice *out there* in this world as well.

Consequently I developed an urge *to do something* – to create change. As a student of International Development at the University of Vienna I was confronted daily with learning about the economic gaps between so-called *developed* and *developing* countries. I heard that development cooperation often results in new dependences. My job as a student has mainly been to occupy myself with issues such as conflicts, poverty and other mind-blowing topics.

---

1 Krishnamurti (2003): 36 Translated by the author. „Aber sehen sie, ohne diese Flamme der Unzufriedenheit werden Sie niemals den Antrieb haben, welcher der Anfang der Kreativität ist."

Retrospectively, I have been through phases of disillusionment, frustration and at times seemingly powerless rage about the condition of our world throughout the past six years. I have been passionately blaming and judging those who I deemed *guilty*. Gradually this desperate anger transformed into the desire to become more conscious about myself and my own participation in this game. In meditation courses I started unveiling the suffering, starvation, violence, greed, oppression and injustice that were and are occurring *inside of me*. Blaming and rage were soon no appropriate options anymore in creating positive change. Transformation through self-awareness has then become more exciting to me than being absorbed in political activism.

This internal journey, incited by a thirst for more consciousness about my fears, needs, hidden motivations and unconscious behaviour patterns led me to the *Peace Studies* program in Innsbruck. I quickly sensed that I had found a community which shared the feeling that inward realisations bring about changes of perspective towards the world outside of oneself. Within the Peace Studies program I was given a framework for something that I already felt intuitively: The concept of *transrational peaces*[2] – which will be explained further on in this book.

Concluding I can state that I started my research-journey from a harbour of thankfulness, manoeuvred by an awaking breeze of critical awareness that there exist innumerable life-realities about which I have not got a clue. Through the means of this research, I want to dive into a life-reality that I have never experienced myself – prison – in order to investigate whether inner freedom can also be sensed in conditions which are possibly not as strengthening, nourishing and supportive as the conditions in which I grew up.

My Disruption

I am *free*. I am free, because I am convinced that it is me who decides, more or less consciously, in which direction my life goes. It is me who attracts and rejects the experiences that I want to make. Free, because I am responsible to create my destiny every day anew.

I am a *prisoner*. I am a prisoner whenever I feel kept in a mental prison-cell, surrounded by borders which I supposedly cannot cross. I long for freedom from socially accepted, constructed behaviour patterns, norms, and mindsets. I feel repressed by collective Do's and Don'ts.

---

2 See Dietrich (2008)

I am an *oppressor*. I am an oppressor whenever I suppress my own desires or thoughts that I have which may be seen as not morally noble – as for example judging others, jealousy, fear – instead of honestly admitting what I feel. Whether I want it or not, I am an oppressor, because simply living in Austria, consuming what has been produced in so-called developing countries by the people who work hard and are not appropriately paid or live in poverty themselves, makes me an oppressor. I am the *oppressed.* I am oppressed when my own fears, doubts or memories keep me from living my full potential in the present. Oppressed, when my patterns bar me from courageously and spontaneously jumping into new adventures. Furthermore I am oppressed on a structural level, as for example being a woman, aware that I will probably not be paid as well as a man doing the same work.

I am an *optimist* who strongly believes in the creative potential of each and every person. I am convinced that human beings do have a compassionate core which wants to love and be loved, but is most of the times buried under a soil of sorrows, desperation, fears of being rejected, emotionally hurt or doubts about one's own unique preciousness. Yet, frequently I feel *disillusioned*, seeing this potential wasted by passivity, dull consumption, and lack of enthusiasm. Whenever I hear stories of brutal, inhuman cruelties that humans are able to commit, I wonder whether my assumption of everybody having a pure core is simply blissfully ignorant.

I am aware that both sides live within me, the free and the prisoner, the oppressed and the oppressor, the optimist and the disillusioned. Therefore all these aspects will be alive in this current work. I will now lighten up the driving force for choosing my specific topic.

A longing for Freedom

I want to be free. Free from imaginary fears and instead full of trust that everything carries the potential for positive change; trusting that life carries, guides, and protects me. Free from the demand that I have to be some way, achieve this or that, have fully developed certain skills, before I am *good enough* and only then can be at peace with myself.

I long for freedom and independence from outer circumstances. Obstacles that frequently hinder people and myself to feel free are the "inner cops"[3]. According

3 See Boal (2006): 138 "Cops in the head" is an expression coined by Augusto Boal in his book "The Rainbow of Desire" and means the inner instances that restrict us. Translated by the author.

to Augusto Boal these are entities "we each have that prevent us from doing something that, objectively, we have every opportunity and skill to do."[4] They are the voices in one's head, which block us from risking more, acting more spontaneously, stepping out of behaviour patterns and exploring new ways of living. In this book I focus on creative alternatives and playful methods of experiencing oneself and thereby possibly discovering spaces of inner freedom.

My Research Interest

Questions on Freedom

In the beginning there was a personal longing for freedom. Out of this desire the questions arose: How much does the realization of inner freedom and inner peace depend on the outer circumstances? Is it me who determines to feel free? Or does somebody else, a society or the *system* destine our freedom and our feelings of oppression?

This brought me to think about the question of freedom inside prisons, which for me is the symbol for the absence of freedom.[5] Consequently more questions came up: Are people in prison automatically less free than those who can move *freely*? Could everyday life be seen as a prison? Do prisons have the potential, by giving space and time, to encourage reflection on inner freedom and the discovery of people's inherent potential? Would the existence of prisons be legitimate without a mindset that judges some as morally superior and others as inferior? If prisoners are adjudged for committing acts of physical violence, is it a sustainable way out of the vicious circle of violence if to conflict emotional violence upon them, the *culprits*, by treating them as the 'black sheeps' of society?

Balance along a paradox

Sharing my idea to write about Theatre in Prison with my friends and family, the most common questions I was asked highlighted one inherent antagonism: Can

4 Boal in Bettencourt (2000)
5 In Austria detainment is also called Freiheitsentzug, which literally means deprivation of freedom.

freedom only be experienced internally, independent of the outer circumstances? If this is the case, prisons would not be an obstacle to freedom. But, if one has to be physically free in order to feel internally free, the effort to discover freedom within prisons through theatre would be in vain. Contemplating on these conflictive arguments, I realized that both are true to a certain extent. On one hand, I can assume that living behind iron bars would deeply affect my sensation of inner freedom. It would probably take an enormous effort to keep my spirits up and to not feel guilty, inferior, frustrated, furious or filled with hatred. It would also be a challenge to discover alternative ways in which I could express myself and experience connectedness to others – while being locked up for up to 24 hours a day.

On the other hand, I have observed that no matter whether it is a cloudy or a sunny day, it is my inner attitude of having a good or a sad day which determines my perception of the weather. Hence, it is my inner freedom and my approach which has the power to make the external conditions appear in a different light. It usually only takes a slight change of perspective; looking at a situation from another angle or in another mood, perhaps and it suddenly transforms from hopelessness to ease, while the outer circumstances in fact remain the same.

This research will balance along these two poles and determining whether there can be inner freedom which does not depend on outer circumstances or as Osho claimed: "Take responsibility! And then even in utter poverty, suffering, imprisoned in a jail, you will remain completely a master of yourself."[6] From this viewpoint a focus on the discovery of a stable inner freedom would be crucial, instead of spending time on fighting outer political, oppressive conditions. Prison critique, from this perspective, would not be as expedient in terms of gaining inner freedom, as practising methods to realize personal, inner freedom.

There is also the argument that there cannot be freedom if one lacks freedom of movement and expression and does not have control to create their own daily life! If the mindset is that freedom is determined by outer conditions, it would obviously have a much greater and more effective impact on the creation of an atmosphere of freedom if prisons were abolished. Meditation, theatre and other methods to discover one's inner potential and a way to gain self-confidence would not be of prior ranking within this standpoint.

The topic of this book has gone through a challenging process of asking: *How can I find a balance between those two poles, those two approaches - the refor-*

---

6 Osho (2004): 34

mative transformation of current conditions (as it would be to bring theatre into prisons) *and the radical question of a make-believe natural system* (by formulating a prison critique).

I think that work ought to be done on both poles, the reformation of current conditions while asking the radical question of why prisons have to exist and at the same time looking out for alternatives. Considering the individuals who live or work in prisons and at the same time considering the structures built to keep this machine running; critiquing the prison system and political measures are as necessary as healing, giving emotional support, and applying methods which allow people to get into a more reflective, respectful relationship with themselves and others.[7]

My Focus

In awareness that both approaches are logical and appropriate I can clearly see my contribution in the elaboration of methods to discover inner freedom which evolves through profound *knowledge of oneself*, *self-esteem* and *connection* to others as well as *trust* in oneself, others and life – joyfully. Still, I appreciate those who put their energy into questioning the existence of prisons and respect those who are eagerly working in the fields of reconciliation and cultivating compassionate alternatives to punishment. Contemplating which framework could be provided within a prison that offers the inmates a chance to playfully experiment with unconscious behaviour-patterns or switch their perspectives for an instance and thereby regain the freedom to have alternative choices – *theatre* came into my mind.

Theatre

I have chosen the element of theatre as a possible method to discover inner freedom for the following reasons. Observation of oneself and others is crucial, if one wants to imitate a character, improvise a situation and act authentically. Apart from sensual observation, deep empathizing is necessary – feeling oneself in a role. Moreover, it is almost impossible not to touch and be touched by others

7 The general impression I got from talks with former inmates, documentary movies and literature was that reflective and respectful relationships between one another and with oneself are rare in prison, though there might of course be exceptional cases.

while acting, physically as well as emotionally. I personally have joined several 'Theatre of the Oppressed'[8]-Workshops and I was astonished how quickly the participants connected and became friends, through acting together for a few days.

The implementation of theatre in prisons acknowledges the fact that prisons exist and tries to work with the potential of this circumstance. "Prisons brutalise and degrade offenders; they shatter self-esteem and good intentions"[9], Jenny Hughes a British prison theatre practitioner, states. Prisons are institutions which have their fundaments in judging and punishing, on the assumption that prisoners failed or are *wrong* in some way; therefore it is important to reach those people, who might already feel as a societal *outcast,* by using methods that facilitate self-confidence.

Most prison inmates have gone through some kind of traumatic experience in their lives before being confined. A long history of pain and frustration might lie behind them and there is often the need for therapeutical healing. Certain theatre methods work with analyzing and releasing the past in order to learn lessons for the future. The understanding of freedom that I am interested in, however, deals with the inner sensation of freedom. Hence, I will not focus on becoming *free from* the past, but rather to feel *free for* living one's creative potential.

Furthermore, I hypothesize that there are two qualities needed in everyday li-fe: *self-reflection* and *connection* to our fellow human beings. As I found both qualities emphasized in the framework of Theatre of the Oppressed, this theatre form has been selected as the one which I will specifically research on.

Theatre of the Oppressed

Theatre of the Oppressed originated from the idea of becoming free of oppressi-on. Solidarity, or as I would call it *the feeling of connection*, with other human beings has always been an inherent value in the Theatre of the Oppressed app-roach. Over the years the methods of Theatre of the Oppressed became increa-singly more introspective, which means they aim more at *self-reflection* and discovery of the oppression one is unknowingly doing to oneself and others.

In this work I deal with the following questions: In which ways does the prac-tise of Theatre of the Oppressed methods enhance trust in oneself, others and life? How do techniques of Theatre of the Oppressed facilitate a participant's

8 Boal (2007): Theatre of the Oppressed
9 Hughes in Thompson (1998): 45

discovery of his or her inherent creativity? Does applying Theatre of the Oppressed to prisons generate critical thinking within the participants, in the sense of scrutinizing the structures that connect their individual fates? In which ways do role playing and the stepping into different characters cultivate empathy within them? Does cooperative theatre work bring about a sense of responsibility for oneself and the group? How do the relationships between inmates transform during the process of doing theatre work together? Does the picture one has about her or himself transform through a process of Theatre of the Oppressed work?

Coined by my own experiences, I believe that Theatre of the Oppressed has the potential to make fundamental, inward changes in a person. It provokes a radical questioning of our blind belief in authorities and tries to give us back the authority over our own lives, in this sense, I see a strong connection to the question of freedom. The relevant research interest is now to find out whether my personal impressions will be confirmed by practitioners and participants who experimented with Theatre of the Oppressed in prison.

Research Question

> In which sense does the application of Theatre of the Oppressed transform the sensation of inner freedom for people living in prison?

Summary of my momentary perspective

The first spark was a longing for personal freedom, which caused the question of whether inner freedom is dependent on outer circumstances. Subsequently prison entered my mind as the symbol for the absence of freedom. Determining which methods would facilitate a sensation of inner freedom, I discovered Theatre as an invaluable method for self-reflection, connection, playful joy and creativity – which for me are crucial aspects of inner freedom. Within the wide fields of theatre I chose to focus on Theatre of the Oppressed, due to its political and socially motivated core. The combination of these elements freedom, prison, and Theatre of the Oppressed, will help me to find out whether inner freedom is possible in prisons; whether Theatre of the Oppressed is an appropriate form to realize this freedom; and whether the inner sensation of freedom transforms through the process of practising Theatre of the Oppressed.

State of the Art

The topic of my research circles around the question of freedom and whether a critical and at the same time creative approach as Theatre of the Oppressed, facilitates the sensation of inner freedom. The settings in which this question is posed are prisons. The literature selected for my query originates from different academic disciplines. The momentary state of the art in the fields relevant for my research is as follows.

To investigate different perspectives on freedom, I selected literature that fits best into the categories of philosophy and spirituality. I developed a definition of freedom strongly inspired by two main *speakers*[10], Jiddu Krishnamurti and Osho. Although both are internationally famous, Krishnamurti's and Osho's thoughts are barely regarded as relevant in European academic discourses. Both grew up in India, studied a variety of spiritual traditions from different parts of the world, and continuously emphasised the importance of reaching beyond mere rationality. These factors might have contributed to a general attitude of doubt in their academic credibility. Regarding them as an enriching source of inspiration when dealing with the question of freedom I will, nevertheless, make them the core of my research on freedom.

Krishnamurti has been brought up by the Theosophical Society which saw in him the prophesied World Teacher. He, however, was consistent in declaring that "Truth is a Pathless Land"[11] and hence refused to take on the role of a spiritual authority, neither did he propose methods on *how* to become free. He gave inspiring, awakening talks on inner freedom, meditation, pedagogy and the liberation from dogmas, traditions, beliefs or authorities – always insisting: "Do not agree with me. Find out for yourself."[12] This expression is crucial for his approach.

Osho, on the other hand, took on the role of a spiritual leader and developed dynamic meditation practises which spread widely in many parts of the world. Osho studied ancient Eastern wisdom-traditions such as Tantra, Shivaism, Yoga,

---

10 Calling them *authors* would not be appropriate as they have never written books themselves. Their innumerable speeches have been taken notes of or were recorded and then published.

11 See Bernie's Home Page: Krishnamurti http://bernie.cncfamily.com/k_pathless.htm

12 Krishnamurti (2003): 19 Translated by the author. "Stimmen Sie mir nicht zu. Finden Sie es heraus."

Taoism, Zen, Buddhism, Sufism, Jaininsm and explained the core of these spiritual streams to people in the so-called West. As university professor of philosophy he was also familiar with European thinkers as Aristotle, Plato, Jean Paul Sartre, Marx and many others. He was a fiercely disputed, provocative speaker, famous for not hesitating to speak out what was on his mind and constantly challenging established *truths*. Compared to Krishnamurti, who talked more about becoming free *from* certain conditionings and structures, Osho emphasised the importance of becoming free *for* something, as for instance creativity and authenticity. A focus on freedom *from* seemed empty to him, lacking beauty and playfulness.

In the field of Peace Studies, both have been categorized as *transrational* peace thinkers by Wolfgang Dietrich.[13] The concept of *transrational* or *transpersonal peaces* is a relevant and new discourse in Peace Studies. The literature used therefore is "Variationen über die vielen Frieden. Band 1: Deutungen" in which Dietrich[14] illustrates different approaches to peace.

Concerning the *theory* of Theatre of the Oppressed the literary sources originate from the fields of study of theatre pedagogy, pedagogy, social work and arts. Augusto Boal was the one who collected a great number of theatre practises, which from his point of view had the potential to liberate from oppression, combined them, and categorized them as 'Theatre of the Oppressed'. As creator of Theatre of the Oppressed, author of six books and innumerable articles on that topic as well as a passionate theatre practitioner – and social activist – for most of his lifetime Boal's writings are fundamental in this field of research.

Paulo Freire constructed the theoretical, conceptual fundament for Augusto Boal's theatrical practise in his "Pedagogy of the Oppressed"[15]. Paolo Freire was a Brazilian pedagogue committed to support the oppressed classes in their struggle for political participation, with the means of education and alphabetisation. Theatre of the Oppressed cannot be discussed without mentioning its connection to Freire. Especially if Theatre of the Oppressed is applied to prisons it is crucial to perceive the prison-inmates as active subjects, as intelligent performers, within a creative process and not as passive objects volunteering to be educated or entertained, as Freire sedulously emphasised.

Francis Babbage's book "Augusto Boal"[16] describes Boal's biographical context that inspired the creation of Theatre of the Oppressed. Stefan Ried's thesis

13 See Dietrich (2008)
14 Dietrich (2008)
15 Freire (1996): Pedagogy of the Oppressed
16 Babbage (2004)

on "Trials to use Augusto Boal's Theatre of the Oppressed as praxis against the tendency of reification of the bourgeois/civil society"[17] provided information about the background of Boal's and Freire's thinking. He explained which personalities and ideas have been influential for Boal. Barbara Frey's[18] thesis pointed out crucial points of critique on the Theatre of the Oppressed.

The systemic approach to social theatre from David Diamond is not elaborated in this research, yet it is certainly an important position within the discourse on Theatre of the Oppressed. Unlike Theatre of the Oppressed by which "Theatre for Living"[19] is strongly inspired, it moves away from the clear division between oppressor and oppressed and tries to shed light on the complexity beyond this duality. Consequently, not only the *oppressed* protagonist can be exchanged, but anyone who someone of the audience can sympathise with.

The literature consulted for the *practical* application of Theatre of the Oppressed to prisons consists of anthologies of Prison Theatre as well as on independent articles by Theatre of the Oppressed practitioners who have experiences in working in prison. Authors of these articles often have a background as actresses or actors, artists, community workers, social/political activists, pedagogues, psychologists, (drama) therapists, academics or others.

James Thompson's "Prison Theatre – Practices and Perspectives in Prison Theatre"[20] and Michael Balfour's "Theatre in Prison – Theory and Practice"[21] serve as my basis literature. Both aim at the combination of theatre and prison and highlight the importance of combining theory and practise. Thompson and Balfour themselves work with Theatre of the Oppressed and combined it with methods of cognitive behaviour theory. Apart from their books, I came across inspiring articles of each of them, which I included in my research.

"Under Pressure" is the international online newsletter about Theatre of the Oppressed and is available at the International Theatre of the Oppressed Homepage[22]. In January 2008, one issue was published which centred on the theme 'Theatre of the Oppressed in prisons'. [23] This issue included articles about projects in Brazil, Italy, the Netherlands, Germany and Croatia and was therefore an important source of my research.

---

17 Ried (2007) Title has been translated by the author.
18 Frey (1989)
19 Diamond (2007)
20 Thompson (1998)
21 Balfour (2004)
22 Under Pressure (2006)
23 Under Pressure (2008)

Generally, I observed that up to now there has not been a published research dealing with the application of Theatre of the Oppressed in prisons. There are several reports on individual projects in different parts of the world, yet no international overview or comparison that describes the broad variety of these projects and their different approaches.

Method and Structure

My research question is "In which sense does the application of Theatre of the Oppressed transform the sensation of inner freedom for people living in prison?" Consequently, the issue arises of how to measure the *sensation of inner freedom*? How can I analyse the transformations occurring throughout the process of practising Theatre of the Oppressed in prisons? Here I will clarify the method of my research and the structure of this book. Before I go deeper in details of my structure, however, I would like to mention one detail of content: choosing a style of avoiding reaffirmation of fixed gender attributions.

Concerning gender in my writing style
Searching for an appropriate way of avoiding to write *he or she* every time when I intend to talk about both sexes, I chose to apply *he* and *she* (or *him* and *her*) totally randomly throughout the whole book.

Definition of Freedom

First of all, I need to develop a definition of inner freedom, which will be used throughout the research. This definition has to establish different criteria which allow assessing whether inner freedom is felt at all and whether it has transformed throughout the theatre process. Thus, the freedom definition ought to have visible, ascertainable features which enable me to measure changes. This will be a challenging task, as inner freedom might appear as a subjective, individually distinctive sensation – ungraspable by objective, general means of measurement. Therefore the definition of freedom needs to leave space for interpretation, while at the same time having clear determinants.

The definition of freedom will be formed by results of literature research. Intrigued in topics of personal, inner freedom, I will not go deeper into connotations of freedom in politics and international relations. I will instead approach the question of inner freedom mainly through philosophical and spiritual literature.

My personal perspective on freedom will serve as a base from which I set off my elaborations. An investigation of the etymological notion of freedom in the German language, *Freiheit*, will follow. Scrutinizing this notion is of importance to me as I have been strongly coined by unconsciously hearing and applying the term *Freiheit* for more than twenty years and never unveiled its intrinsic, culturally determined messages. Before going in depth with Krishnamurti and Osho, I will explain the concept of *transrational* or *transpersonal peaces* as elaborated by Wolfgang Dietrich. In order to embed Krishnamurti's and Osho's perspectives on freedom into the discipline of Peace Studies, they will be categorized as *transrational* freedom thinkers.

"Freedom from the Known"[24] by Krishnamurti impressed me with its challenging radicalness and the persistent calling to observe my thoughts – neither judging nor accepting them. His words feel true to me, as I do not see any ornaments, sweet-talking or falsehood. He did not want to be blindly believed or honoured and he consistently refused the status of a (spiritual) authority. These aspects were the reason to choose him as one authentic speaker from which to learn about inner freedom.

The second, in my opinion authentic speaker on freedom is Osho. "Freedom – The Courage to be Yourself"[25] has enriched me with two essential ideas. Firstly, the idea to distinguish between freedom *from* and freedom *for*; Secondly, to perceive freedom as the courage to be yourself, hence freedom is to regain one's authenticity.

From these approaches I filter certain criteria, which will then form an appropriate freedom definition. Thus, the method for this chapter on Freedom will be literature research and analysis of communalities and contradictions.

Literature Research on "Theatre of the Oppressed"

The subsequent chapter will offer an introduction into Theatre of the Oppressed. The method chosen for this endeavour will again be literature research, using mainly books written by or on Augusto Boal and Paulo Freire. Boal and Freire

---

24 Krishnamurti (1969)
25 Osho (2004)

will be my main references when investigating origin, philosophy and methods of Theatre of the Oppressed.I will furthermore integrate reports and experiences from other Theatre of the Oppressed practitioners and thereby add a greater variety of perspectives on this topic. Within this chapter I want to light up the general approach of Theatre of the Oppressed in order to communicate my argumentation of its transformative potential. This part is crucial, as it functions to depict a clear picture of Theatre of the Oppressed, before I continue to go in depth with its application to prisons.

What I personally read as the essence of Boal's approach, as the unshakably stable element that remained throughout a course of life with many changes, is the conviction that: *Everybody is creative; Everybody is an actor or actress; Everybody has the potential to make a difference in the world.* As theatre maker and social activist, he has sought to combine two fundamental elements which are crucial in this book: Creativity and social/political change.

In order to construct an associative bridge between the chapters 'Freedom' and 'Theatre of the Oppressed', I will shortly overview communalities as well as contradictions between my definition of freedom – inspired by Krishnamurti and Osho – and the understanding of freedom within the Theatre of the Oppressed. For this chapter, 'Theatre of the Oppressed and Freedom', no additional literature has been consulted, but my personal thoughts functioned to combine and contrast them with each other.

Literature research on Theatre of the Oppressed in Prison

The literature used for this endeavour, consists mainly of anthologies of articles on prison theatre projects conducted in different parts of the world by different theatre practitioners. This variety of perspectives gives impressions of manifold approaches and ways of realization. Out of these books I selected articles that explicitly referred to Theatre of the Oppressed.

Additionally to the anthologies published by James Thompson and Michael Balfour I searched for independent articles by other practitioners which documented their experiences with Theatre of the Oppressed in prison. Some of them evaluated the effects, others described the applied methods in more detail and still others contained quotes and impressions of workshop participants, hence prisoners, themselves. Especially the articles of Katrin Wolf and Till Baumann in Germany, Sonja Kuftinec and Chen Alon in Israel, Michael Bettencourt in the USA, Ronald Matthijssen in the Netherlands, and Jenny Hughes writing for the TiPP centre in Great Britain, have been invaluable to me.

I have initially planned to enrich this research by conducting a case-study. However, I discovered that in the months of my research and writing process there would not be a Theatre of the Oppressed prison project in the process of realisation in an English or German speaking country in Europe. (If there was, I did not succeed in locating one on time.) Hence, the chosen method for this part will be literature research, basing on documented experiences by Theatre of the Oppressed practitioners.

Although it would have been my preference to observe the inmate's sensation of freedom myself and assess changes through interviews and questionnaires, due to the non-existence of an actual project, I am bound to primarily investigating what the authors of these articles observed as changes in themselves and in the participants. This method implies a fundamental contradiction to the content of my research. The applied literature is mainly written by theatre practitioners and workshop-leaders and hardly ever by the participating prison-inmates themselves. According to Paulo Freire it is crucial to talk *with* the people – the *oppressed* – about their concerns, thoughts, feelings and not *about* them; to listen to their experiences, and not assuming what they might have experienced.[26] The crux of the matter is: Who is speaking on whose behalf: Is it the *artist* explaining the *participant's* experiences, or does everyone have the chance to express one's own impressions? I am aware that this problem comes along with the difficulty to find detailed documentation on these projects.

In general prison theatre projects often lack evaluation after the artistic process has finished. This brings about the drawback that artists do not have sufficient credible, scientifically proved arguments in favour of the application of Theatre of the Oppressed to prisons at hand and that "excellent projects have disappeared at least in part because of the absence of evidence supporting their usefulness."[27]

I will conclude this chapter by adding a short insertion about prison-critique, from my own point of view. As Theatre of the Oppressed carries the inherent motivation to reveal oppressive structures which are unconsciously accepted or deemed as natural, it is inevitable for me to make a general prison critique. The sources of this sub-chapter will be my personal, collected impressions. Talks with ex-prisoners and guards as well as points of critique which I repeatedly came across in literature written by artists and/or social activists, greatly influenced my personal perspective.

---

26 See Freire (1996)
27 Balfour and Poole in Thompson (1998): 221

Drawing conclusions

The literature on Theatre of the Oppressed applied to prisons will give me insights to evaluate whether the sensation of inner freedom has perceivably transformed throughout the theatre process. The method to conduct a coherent analysis will be as follows. I take the freedom definition elaborated beforehand, and detect few essential key-words. In the literature research I especially observe whether these criteria – these key-words – are explicitly given attention and if changes in these criteria are mentioned. The major part of my evaluation will be my personal interpretation according to what I read between the lines.

FREEDOM

Introduction

In order to create a definition of freedom with which I can work throughout this research and which allows me to evaluate changes in terms of 'inner freedom' for participants of a Theatre of the Oppressed process, I will first need to look at freedom from different perspectives.

I will depict my personal perspective at the beginning in order to clarify the inherent ideas I set off; to share with you the more or less conscious perspective from which I shed light on everything that follows. In a second step the etymological notion of freedom in the German language will be elaborated. This is crucial, as this notion has certainly been instilled subtly into my understandings of freedom by the language/culture that surrounds me. Before dealing with the two *transrational* freedom thinkers, Krishnamurti and Osho, I will shortly explain Dietrich's concept of *transrational/transpersonal peaces* in order to embed my research into the discipline of Peace Studies. Subsequently Jiddu Krishnamurti's and Osho's perspectives on freedom will be introduced.

All these perspectives will then flow into the final chapter in which communalities and differences are analysed. The common and crucial facets of freedom will ultimately form a working definition of 'freedom' that will accompany me throughout this current work.

FREEDOM FROM MY PERSONAL PERSPECTIVE

> Freedom means the capability to say yes when yes is needed, to say no when no is needed, and sometimes to keep quiet when nothing is needed – to be silent, not to say anything. When all these dimensions are available, there is freedom.[28]

The implicit crux about this statement is another criterion for freedom: Only you yourself can decide whether a 'yes', a 'no', or silence is needed in a given mo-

---

28 Osho (2004): Foreword *v*

ment. There is, hopefully, no one who can take this responsibility from you. Freedom, in the above quote, is the absolute self-responsibility after having invigorated the inner courage to speak out an honest 'yes', a straightforward 'no' or having discovered the space of silence for oneself – where there is no shame, no discomfort, no awkwardness in not speaking.

Coming back to my personal perspective of freedom, I would like to explain why I started with this quote of Osho. Before coming across this quote, I had two fundamental poles in my mind when I reflected on freedom: *Trust* and *Critical Thinking*.

When I talk about trust, I do not mean naivety. I do not appreciate it as trust, if a person says 'yes' to everything as a result of not daring to reject. Swallowing and ignoring feelings of disagreement in order to keep up an illusory harmony is not trust for me either.

On the other hand, critical thinking to me is not to equate with mistrust towards everything, but rather the effort of always lighting up and understanding the different facets of an issue and only then get a conscious opinion about it. Critical thinking for me is not a chronic attitude of resistance, which not always arises out of awareness, but out of frustration towards wo/mankind.

In the following chapters I will elaborate the essence of my understanding of freedom along the lines of trust and critical thinking, as these are the poles I try to balance and often struggle. The chapter of trust will be divided into the three sub-chapters of trust in myself, trust in others and trust in life.

Trust

Trust in myself

Trust in myself, means that I dare living my life the way I wish. Hence, I would rarely be bothered by thoughts such as "What might others think about me?", "If I continue to follow my intuition, I may end up on the streets, homeless, without a job or all alone without friends.", "I might fail.", "Maybe if I live this dream I might lose everybody I love.", "Maybe I will not be able to fulfil this task properly.", "Maybe I should wait until I am really good enough in this and only then, when I am excellent, dare to go out to show or teach it to others." "Maybe somebody will be much, much better in this than I could ever be.", "I might physically hurt myself.", "Somebody else might hurt me."

All these doubts about my own capabilities oppress me. These fears restrain me from living my dreams and my inherent potential. They curtail my creativity and my courage to put ideas into practise. Thus, truly trusting in myself opens up an enormous space of freedom within me; a freedom allowing me to live my life in my way.

Honest trust in myself creates a stable self-confidence which no one can disturb. No matter whether I receive a compliment or an offence, I am aware of my own value and do not need anyone to convince or unsettle me about that. Additionally, I would be more indifferent about what is considered fashionable, beautiful or morally acceptable.

I do not claim that I have realized these attitudes, although there are single moments when I feel a complete trust in myself with little worries about external influences, but these moments are rare and usually go by quickly. This feeling, for me is the freedom of no longer being the cue ball of everybody else's opinion, desires or other external influences.

Trusting in myself empowers me with a freedom in which I cease to be a victim of other people's actions. Trusting that I act out of my best intentions and abilities, frees me from sore-consciousness and feelings of guilt. Therefore I stop self-blaming for what I was not able to do, for not succeeding, or for hurting somebody and instead, I forgive myself with the wisdom that I did the best I could in that very moment. Trusting in myself does not mean to become isolated from the community I live in. However, a bit of self-sufficient trust allows me to relate with people out of a desire to truly meet them, rather than out of neediness.

Trust in others

I try to give this trust to others and keep the attitude that everyone acts out of her best intention, or at least in the best way that is possible at the very moment. I endeavour to trust that a person does not want to do me any harm unless I know the contrary to be true. Such instances may be to not speculate whether a person's compliment was genuine or to not speculate on others *true motivations*, but to either believe in their honesty and their will to be good people or to directly confront this person with my suspicion. This, in my opinion, is much better than drawing conclusions.

I believe that every act of offence is a way of expressing a need. For example, what might appear as an affront, threat or envy might originate from a need to be loved and accepted. Therefore it makes great sense to me to work with alternative, non-violent ways to express needs such as theatre acting, dancing, arts, writing, speaking or music. I expect the methods of Theatre of the Oppressed to enable me and others to recognize needs and formulate them in an open way, without hurting anyone – neither physically nor emotionally. To trust in others also means to trust in the potential of others, even though that potential might not be fully lived yet – just as one's own, probably.

Trust in life

Whatever happens, I seek to keep an underlying, profound trust in life. Feeling that everything will turn out fine; confiding that whatever does not make any sense in this moment will make sense sooner or later – maybe I simply need some distance.

Trusting that everything that happens has the potential to turn into something better; Trusting that I am, at the same time, an extremely tiny particle of the universe and it is beyond my power to grasp the whole mystery, however, knowing that everything is connected, I do have an influence on the whole. Relying on the possibility that anything I un/consciously wish to enter into my life, every experience I want to make, might come true. Trust means to stop complaining and no longer exist in victim mode, and become an active participant in life's correlations with the confidence to invite experiences into my life.

Trust in life from my point of view also means having the wisdom that every state of mind and every mood will go by, change, and vanish. I experience confusion, happiness, sadness, chaos, delightedness, joy, light heartedness, desperation, envy, and pride, but no matter how eternal these emotions might feel, I know that they will change at one point to another condition. So, having the trust that when I feel terrible it will pass, and when I feel great it will vanish– I can still remain humorous about it. However, frankly admitted, quite often I am sitting in life's rollercoaster, with my head stuck in the dark rain clouds of chaos, far from taking anything with humorous ease.

Critical Thinking

Apart from trusting in life and saying a passionate 'yes' from the bottom of the heart to life's teachings, only together with the courage to say 'no' can there be a more complete freedom. I trust that everything which occurs in my life has a deeper sense and is a lesson for me to learn from.

On the other hand there is the ability to think critically, to scrutinize for example an oppressive situation and dare to say "No, I/we do not want this!" The before mentioned concept of trust can easily be misunderstood by believing that *everything has to be accepted.* I struggle occasionally when it comes to saying "No!" At times, it is difficult to be against something, to ruthlessly dissect and criticize it, to stand up against it. However, I am convinced that freedom can only be there if the sphere of disapproval is conquered and from then on can be visited whenever it is needed.

Saying 'no' to structures that are discriminating because they take away the possibilities for personal growth; and rebelling against systems that deprive people of their basic needs or their creative potential, without becoming a cheerless, frustrated misanthrope – that is what I call critical thinking. Critical thinking from my point of view is the clarity to know when I/we no longer want to participate in a game that I/we find absurd.

Critical thinking, as I understand it, evolves from the realisation that "I am a part of the whole, and I cannot find the 'I' separated from the rest of humanity"[29]. Hence, being conscious that I am a responsible part of the whole leads to the necessity for critically scrutinizing what is generally accepted as truth.

Summary of my personal perspective on freedom

Freedom is to trust in myself and in life – and with this inner confidence go wherever I decide to go. At the same time, freedom is to not be fooled by people or systems that dictate moral norms and codes of behaviour, create beauty standards, materialistic desires or ideas of how a person should be, in order to be of value.

These two poles appear as a paradox. However, I am convinced that in order to sense a freedom that enables enthusiastic playfulness and trustful, childlike spontaneity, there must be at the same time a critical process of liberation from numbing, imprisoning, and societal structures. Critical thinking can generate profound disillusionment, which might allow for one's true thoughts and feelings to be unmasked.

In the following chapter the etymological notion of freedom in the German language, *Freiheit*, will be elaborated. Scrutinizing this notion is relevant to me as I have been strongly coined by unconsciously hearing and applying the term *Freiheit* for all my life and never unveiled its intrinsic, culturally determined messages.

29 M.K. Ghandi Institute for Nonviolence in Dietrich (2008): 326 Translated by the author.

THE ETYMOLOGICAL NOTION OF *FREIHEIT*, FREEDOM, IN GERMAN

My mother tongue is German. Therefore I will analyze the etymological notion of the adjective *frei*, free and its noun *Freiheit*, freedom. Before going into details on the development of these terms throughout the ages, I deem it necessary to give a short overview about the chronological context of the languages I am talking about.

Indo-European, or Indo-Germanic, was spoken in the 3rd millennium B.C. in central Europe. From then on some of these peoples spread all over Europe and reached the area of what we call India today. The Indo-European language has been influenced and transformed by migration, conquest, assimilation and other factors.[30] One branch of it developed into Old High German which refers to the period between the 8th and the 11th century in central Europe. Middle High German denotes the time span between the 12th and the 15th century, whereas New High German has been practised from the 16th century until the present.[31]

The roots of the term *frei*

Free in the sense of loving, beloved, dear and caring for someone

The term *frei* originated from meaning beloved, dear, good and lovely. The Indo-European roots *prai* and *pri* stood for liking someone, treating someone with care or having a peaceful and merry attitude. In Old Indian the root *priyáh* described something that was dear to one, beloved or owned. A similar Old Indian expression, *prinati*, denoted being delighted, amused and animated or enjoying something.[32] The notion of the Old Indo-Germanic term *priió* was beloved and lovely, *pritá* stood for friendly.[33] Apart from loving, the Indo-European root *prai* furthermore meant to protect, provide shelter and care for someone.[34]

30 Duden – Das Herkunftswörterbuch (2007): 164
31 Duden – Das Herkunftswörterbuch (2007): 9
32 Etymologisches Wörterbuch des Deutschen (2005): 372
33 Etymologisches Wörterbuch es Althochdeutschen (2007): 555f
34 Duden – Das Herkunftswörterbuch (2007): 235

Firstly, we see that all roots of the term *frei* originally had positive connotations. Friendly, beloved, amused, delighted, lovely, dear, caring and protecting are adjectives that describe a desirable state. Secondly, within these origins, a separation can be discovered, between people who were dear and others who were strangers. Those who belonged to one's own kin were precious, so they had to be protected and cared for. Relatives, loved ones and friends were called the *free* ones, because they were welcome and thus free within the community. On the other hand there have been the foreigners, slaves or bond-men that were not part of the family or clan hence they would not be cared for in the same way.[35] It seems that being free in those days has been an exclusive privilege for people who belonged to a group and had been granted certain rights. They were loved, welcomed and would be sheltered. Foreigners and slaves, on the other hand, did not enjoy the same privileges.

Freeing someone meant to love and court somebody

From the roots *prai* and *pri* the Old High German term *fri* arose. In the Gothic language *frijon* meant to love or to free someone. Freeing a person was understood as wanting to espouse and court him. Interestingly in this context freeing another person meant to marry her, which in other words could as well be called making a commitment or getting engaged, whereas in other contexts being free stood for being unbound, disengaged or even immoral and impertinent.[36]

These two notions seem rather contrary from my point of view. The first notion claims that being free goes together with loving, caring for, protecting and marrying or taking possession of something or someone. The second notion seemingly says the opposite. Being free means to be unbound and not owned by anyone. One further example for the second notion would be that in the Old Saxon language a free woman was called *fri* and described a woman belonging to herself.[37]

---

35 Duden – Das Herkunftswörterbuch (2007): 235
36 Grimm, Jacob und Wilhelm (1854): frei
37 Grimm, Jacob und Wilhelm (1854): frei

The roots of the *term Freiheit*

Freiheit originally meant to have a 'free neck'.
Freiheit originates from the Old High German term *frihalsi*, in Latin *collum liberum*, describing a "free neck".[38] One interpretation is that one who does not have a neck burdened by chains is free. Another interpretation would be that one is free who has the power to decide over his own neck. It was beyond the slave's and bondmen's power to protect their own necks from violence and beheading by their masters. The landlords had the power to decapitate their slaves whenever they deemed it necessary – but the landlords themselves had free necks, free from the danger of anyone else decapitating them.[39]

Freiheit came from *frihalsi*, later on in Old High German it changes into *friheit*. In those days *friheit* referred to a granted privilege. In New High German it was *vriheit*, which named a privileged area, such as a free place in front of an official building. From then on it developed into *freiheit*.[40]

Freedom and its connection to peace

Freidjan in the Gothic language meant to protect and provide shelter. Here the correlation to *Friedhof* appears. (*Friede-* means peace and *-hof* can be translated by yard.) *Friedhof* is the German term for graveyard, a protected, sheltered place for the beloved, dear people. In Old-High-German *fridu* means protection and peace. This is interesting, because here we see a strong connection between freedom, *Freiheit*, and peace, *Friede*.[41]

> The meaning of *frei* is in turn etymologically derived from *priya* for *eigen* (own), but also *near* (nahe) and *lieb* (dear, beloved).
>
> The *Eigene* (own) as point of reference for the *friedlich* (peaceful) can not be understood in the modern or legal-Roman sense as that to which one has a legal title, but it is about that which one has produced oneself.[42] (Dietrich, 2008)

38 Grimm, Jacob und Wilhelm (1854): Freiheit
39 Etymologisches Wörterbuch es Althochdeutschen (2007): 565
40 Duden – Das Herkunftswörterbuch (2007): 235
41 Duden – Das Herkunftswörterbuch (2007): 235
42 Dietrich (2008): 159 Translated by Dietrich in a lecture at the MA Program for Peace Studies in Innsbruck.

This quote clarifies that originally those beloved, close people as well as the items which one had produced herself were connected to the *owner* through bonds of affection and familiarity and not due to purchasing or conquering them.

Summary of the etymological notion of freedom in German

The term *frei*, free, originally meant to love, being dear to one, caring for, protecting and owning. These bonds of affection and familiarity were a privilege to one's own kin. Originally, *frei* had described relationships between people. Yet, in the course of time the German peoples added a legal notion of being *free* to reflect an emotional content.[43]

An interesting contradiction that caught my eye is the following. On the one hand freeing someone meant to marry, to own someone, hence, to establish an institutional bond. On the other hand freedom was understood as the opposite to being bound, namely being free from bonds and engagement. A free woman or men was free in the sense of not being engaged or possessed.

Freedom came from having a "free neck". Here again, freedom was a privilege owned by the masters, not by the slaves. Furthermore, this brings me to a personal consideration. The picture of a neck burdened with chains describes the physical manifestation of not being free. I wonder whether today, on a more subtle level it could be seen as the absence of freedom, if the breath does not flow smoothly through the neck. If the neck is burdened by energetic blockades, if one has a tensed neck or a headache about something would that not also be a sign of not being free?

Interestingly the words *Freiheit*, freedom, and *Friede*, peace, have the same roots. Both come from something or someone being near and dear, belonging to one's own kin and should be protected.

Speaking of the connection between freedom and peace, the following chapter will connect the perspectives of Jiddu Krishnamurti and Osho on freedom to the fields of Peace Studies. Therefore, their ideas of freedom will be embedded into Wolfgang Dietrich's category of *transrational* (or *transpersonal*) peace thinkers.

---

43 Duden – Das Herkunftswörterbuch (2007): 235

TRANSRATIONAL AND *TRANSPERSONAL* APPROACHES TO PEACE*S* AND FREEDOM

I have selected Jiddu Krishnamurti and Osho as the two main characters that inspire my definition of freedom. I will deal in depth with their biographies and teachings further on, however certain communalities shall be mentioned beforehand. Both were born in India, lived and held speeches in Europe or the United States for several years and, in the fields of Peace Studies, both have been categorized as representatives for a *transrational* approach, by Wolfgang Dietrich. Dietrich is an Austrian peace researcher who – apart from founding the MA Program for Peace Studies in Innsbruck, Austria – developed the concept of *transrational peaces* in his book "Variationen über die vielen Frieden. Band 1: Deutungen".[44] In order to clarify what is meant by *transrational peaces*, which consequently serves to embed Krishnamurti and Osho into the context of Peace Studies, I will now give a short explanation.

Transrational world views build "on the unity of the Universal or the Cosmic with the individual. They cannot comprehend the subject-object division of modernity."45 Tranrationality is not a meta-physic which is unconscious of rationality, but a conscious transcendence of the boundaries of rationality.46 A transrational perspective values rationality as crucially important, while being aware of its boundaries. Hence, it acknowledges a reality beyond our capability of perceiving it with our senses, to measure it or to prove it.

Transpersonal psychology, founded by Stanislav Grof and Abraham Maslow in the 1970s, focuses on experiences that transcend the biographical boundaries of a person. Key assumptions of their findings are that the source of peace is inside, all existence is cross-linked and connected and every part contains the whole.[47]

Transrational and *transpersonal* approaches generally do not negate, condemn or exclude certain aspects from our lives and our characters such as fear, anger, aggression or sexuality. From these perspectives it is only by becoming fully conscious about these facets that one can gradually move beyond them. "It

44 Dietrich (2008) This book has not yet been translated from German to English. The literal translation of the book title would be: 'Variations of the many peaces. Volume 1: Interpretations'
45 Dietrich (2008): 356 Translated by the author.
46 See Dietrich (2008): 320
47 See Dietrich (2008): 383 Translated by the author.

is not about the *moral* or ascetic oppression of affects which are defined to be negative or uncivilised, but about the conscious and acknowledging balance which is perceived as love, empathy, charity or *agape*."[48] Love and empathy do not come from moral commandments, but arise from the authentic insight that everyone and everything is connected.

One further crucial element of transrational visions of peace is that they "relate to processes at present, to those sensations which occur in the famous Here and Now. This is important for Peace Studies, as peaces, in order to be real ought to be perceived and felt."[49]

Jiddu Krishnamurti and Osho clearly fit into this category of peace approaches – even though both passionately avoided all kinds of categorisations – for various reasons: They argued rationally in their speeches, yet they moved beyond mere rationality in their world views, by promoting meditation, and in Osho's case by developing dynamic meditation practises. Both claimed that the oppression of characteristics which are judged as negative or immoral is rather sanctimonious than wise. One ought to face these facets instead of ignoring them and it is only through consciousness that they can be transformed. Most essential is possibly the fact that Krishnamurti and Osho have always emphasised the power of the Here and Now – as only in this very instance true peace, or freedom, can be experienced. In the following chapters I will elaborate Krishnamurti's and Osho's understandings of *freedom*.

MY INTERPRETATION OF KRISHNAMURTI'S IDEAS OF FREEDOM

Jiddu Krishnamurti was born in 1895 in India and died in 1986 in California, USA. He was discovered and brought to England as a 17 year old by the Theosophical Society which saw him as the prophesied World Teacher. The Theosophical Society, founded in 1875, could be seen as "civil society peace community of the 19th century. Its declared goal was, apart from the investigation of the

48 Dietrich (2008): 368f Translated by the author.
49 Dietrich (2008): 378 Translated by the author.

unexplained laws of nature, to establish a universal brotherhood of humans regardless of race, faith, sex or caste."[50]

Annie Besant and C.W. Leadbeater were Krishnamurti's educators and made him the head of "*The Order of the Star*, the section of the Theosophical Society devoted to the coming of the World Teacher"[51], which he himself dissolved in 1929 with his famous speech "Truth is a Pathless Land"[52]. From then on he spent "the rest of his life travelling the world as an individual speaker and educator on the workings of the human mind."[53] The biographical fact, that he was born in India into a Hindu Brahman family and then, from his teenage years onwards educated by European Theosophists contributed to his ability to take energetic concepts from the Indian culture and respond to them with European critical rationality. However, he rose beyond both perspectives and managed to reach diverse audiences.

Krishnamurti gave innumerable talks on inner freedom, meditation, pedagogy and the liberation from dogmas and traditions. Masses of people labelled him as *enlightened soul*, *saviour of mankind* or *spiritual guru*. However, he never offered any methods. He had been a critic of spiritual paths, because he perceived them as dead, fixed, numb, rigid and inflexible, whereas life for him was something living, moving, dynamic and unpredictable. "Krishnamurti became a radical critic of religious or governmental institutionalism, opponent of any form of dogmatism and representative of a holistic worldview, which perceives the unity of all things in a *transpersonal* sense."[54]

These insights ought to be embedded in the context of Krishnamurti's life. He experienced the problems of institutions and dogmas, as he himself was oppressed by them. Beginning in his early years the Theosophist Society inculcated their ideologies and their visions for him as a *World Teacher*. He eventually rose above the need for a guru, a teacher and a spiritual path after more than 20 years of learning from his teachers and being taught certain methods. Therefore, his critique against the urge to devote oneself to spiritual teachers originates from his own experiences and the realisation that this authoritarian dependence did not free him. Although I largely agree with his critique on authorities and the blind reliance on spiritual guru's and path's, I think that we would immediately fall

50 Dietrich (2008): 332 Translated by the author.
51 Katinka Hesselink: The Life of Jiddu Krishnamurti
52 See Bernie's Home Page: Krishnamurti http://bernie.cncfamily.com/k_pathless.htm
53 Katinka Hesselink: The Life of Jiddu Krishnamurti
54 Dietrich (2008): 333 Translated by the author.

into the same trap again, if we followed Krishnamurti blindly in this view, which resulted from his own life experience and need not be valid for everyone.

He proposed to "explode from the centre"[55], in the sense of freeing oneself immediately from the past, the known and all conditioning, in order to "deal with the totality of life, not only with fragments"[56]. Therefore he disputed the idea of *gradually* discovering more about oneself, or by changing *step by step* via a certain technique, as this would lead to another fragmentation of the whole or to a new dependence on a technique.

He puts it as if it were the simplest thing to *just be in the moment* and to *only face yourself, your anger, your fear without escaping*. It is not easy – for me at least. I observed myself longing for a method. At times it has been a frustrating hardship. For several hours or days, mostly right after reading him, I struggled to remind myself about scrutinizing and looking at myself. I discovered my difficulties to watch, see, listen, hear, feel or taste something with complete attention and not allow distractions to interfere into these observations. I noticed how I created certain strategies to escape from the moment: I would design my far future, plan the following evenings, and dream away to beautiful moments in the last years, amongst many others.

Aware of the people's struggles and innumerable, desperate questions on "*how* to..." Krishnamurti has been consistent in not teaching a path to follow. He was consistent in not declaring himself an authority. He did not want people to believe him, but inspired them to experience and discover for themselves. Personally, I had to realize that in order to follow his teachings consistently, I must question his authority in my mind as well. Therefore, even though he says having a method is inappropriate, this might not be valid for everyone.

Krishnamurti was radical, in the sense of going straight to the roots. His words feel true to me, as I do not see any ornaments, sweet-talking or falsehood. He did not want to convert his audience or make them honour him. These are the reasons why I chose to use his understanding of freedom within my survey. This chapter deals with crucial facets that belong to Krishnamurti's approach to freedom. They will essentially be authority, spontaneity, the here and now, uncertainty, a free flow of energy and finally the commitment to freedom.

---

55 Krishnamurti (1969): 11
56 Krishnamurti (1969): 16

Freedom is beyond authority

Freedom is beyond authority, no matter if it pertains to inner or outer authority. Outer authority would be teachers, parents, gurus, politicians, scientists and others who claim to possess truth. Inner authorities could be accumulated ideas, knowledge, fixed opinions or memories of the past, basically thoughts that prevent one from being fully present in the moment.

Both, inner and outer authorities, stand in between one's authentic self and one's perception of reality. Due to these authorities, reality is not seen with fresh, innocent eyes but rather through prefabricated glasses which determine how reality looks. These authorities mostly understand life within a convinced, stubborn framework and not with a flexible, humble mind that is aware of its ignorance. Such authorities, inside and outside of us, condemn us to live in a fiction where we repeatedly perceive reality through concepts, norms, rules, moral values or dualities such as right and wrong. Consequently, our minds are not fresh enough to find out what is true every moment anew, but tend to get stuck on what they believe to know.

Krishnamurti opposed the need for worldly authorities, as well as for spiritual masters and gurus, who promise to lead their followers to truth. He affirmed that it was only possible to become free if one deconstructs all bonding dependences upon people or institutions which are supposedly wiser, better or more knowledgeable – and thereby starts thinking for herself. "Be one's own leader and one's own disciple"[57] was one statement in which he stressed the emancipation from outside teachers.

"To be free of all authority, of your own and that of another, is to die to everything of yesterday, so that your mind is always fresh, always young, innocent, full of vigour and passion."[58] These words lead towards the next criteria of Krishnamurti's understanding of freedom: Freedom as spontaneity and open-mindedness.

Freedom is spontaneous, open-minded, unprejudiced perception

Dying to yesterday by getting rid of inner and outer authorities implies being spontaneous in perception and unburdened by the past. Freedom in this context is to have the clarity to truly sense, without any expectation of what it will be

57 Krishnamurti (1969): 16
58 Krishnamurti (1969): 19

like, without a judgement whether something feels good or bad and without any projection into the future such as “When will I have it again?” Freedom is to let oneself be surprised by every experience and going into it as if it was the very first time – totally new and unknowing. Freedom is to let go of each experience after it has passed, whether it was pleasant or terrible; Not getting stuck with it; Not carrying on by complaining about it, desiring it to happen again, but being fully in the new moment. Dying to the known must not be misinterpreted as forgetting basic knowledge which is necessary for everyday life – opening a door, cooking food or driving a bike – but to apply this valuable knowledge with consciousness.

Freedom is to be in the *Here* and *Now*

“When you are confronted with something immediately there is no fear. It is only when thought comes in that there is fear.”[59] Krishnamurti says that if one is totally in the Here and Now, there would not be fear, jealousy or anger. There is neither a thought that remembers the past and therefore seeks revenge or feels mistreated, nor a thought that projects its desires into the future and then becomes anxious from lacking something it wants. “To live completely, fully, in the moment is to live with what is, the actual, without any sense of condemnation or justification – then you understand it so totally that you are finished with it. When you see clearly, the problem is solved.”[60] If one is fully present in the moment and open to anything new and unknown, obviously he does not have any certainty of what will happen next.

Freedom is uncertainty, humility, simplicity and inward poverty[61]

In Krishnamurti’s view of freedom there is no certainty. If every moment is free from the known there cannot be a fixed truth that remains stable and is valid in any situation. If one is unburdened by the past this person would not be capable to say “I know for sure”. Fixed, static ideas of oneself, others, things and nature would crumble away in the perpetual changes of life. From the insight that one does not have any answers, maybe a certain humility and innocence would arise,

59 Krishnamurti (1969): 44
60 Krishnamurti (1969): 56
61 Krishnamurti (1969): 24

admitting as Socrates did, "to know nothing at all except that he knows nothing."[62] Furthermore a humble attitude may give birth to a "simplicity that can look directly at things without fear – that can look at ourselves as we actually are without any distortion – to say when we lie we lie, not cover it up or run away from it".[63] Simplicity and inward poverty seem to have a similar meaning for Krishnamurti.

> Poverty is to be completely free of society, though one may have a few more clothes, a few more meals – good God, who cares? [...] Poverty is the most marvellously beautiful thing when the mind is free of society. One must become poor inwardly for then there is no seeking, no asking, no desire, no- nothing! It is only this inward poverty that can see the truth of a life in which there is no conflict at all.[64]

"When there is freedom there is energy"[65]

If we are no longer burdened, blocked, blinded by the concepts which stand just like walls between us and the reality then the energy can flow freely and enable us to see more clearly. It is a waste of energy to keep these concepts alive.

> When you reject something false which you have been carrying about you for generations, when you throw off a burden of any kind, what takes place? You have more energy, haven't you? [...] We need a tremendous amount of energy and we dissipate it through fear but when there is this energy which comes from throwing off every form of fear, that energy itself produces the radical inward revolution.[66]

This sounds logical to me, as it is the same with food. Digesting food is what the body spends a lot of energy on. When I ate less or fasted for some time, after a while I did not feel that hungry anymore and needed a smaller amount of food, while at the same time having more energy. In both cases the reduction of useless ballast sets energy free. Bodies and minds are no longer occupied by heavy psychological or physical loads and therefore freer for being in the moment.

62 Socrates on Washington State University (1996)
63 Krishnamurti (1969): 24
64 Krishnamurti (1969): 60
65 Krishnamurti (1969): 19
66 Krishnamurti (1969): 18

Commitment to freedom

In order to be free, one has to feel a necessity, an inner urge to become free. Krishnamurti formulates that in a quote that I understand as a commitment to freedom.

> Let us state it again clearly: I see I must change completely from the roots of my being; I can no longer depend on any tradition because tradition has brought about this colossal laziness, acceptance and obedience; I cannot possibly look at another to help me to change, not to any teacher, any God, any belief, any system, any outside pressure or influence. What then takes place?[67]

As Krishnamurti emphasised that the willing determination of an individual is needed in order to become free, I would like to summarize my personal interpretation of his teachings.

Summary of Krishnamurti's perspective on freedom

The most essential elements of Jiddu Krishnamurti's understanding of freedom are, in my opinion, the following: Firstly, the freedom from inner and outer authorities and thereby regaining self-responsibility. Secondly, if one becomes free from so-called truths, which is becoming free from the known, this leads to a fresh, spontaneous perception and a state of being in the *here* and *now*. Krishnamurti inexhaustibly speaks about becoming free, conscious, and enlightened within a moment. He claimed that there is no need for a spiritual path, a master or any system that shows the way to freedom for the individual, as this would create new dependences on new authorities that hinder us to discover personally. As Krishnamurti stressed that freedom does not occur to one gradually but within one single instant he was consistent in never proposing a spiritual path or method one has to follow.

Even though he might be absolutely right and freedom may all of a sudden fall from the sky onto my head, for me however the interesting question is not whether this is possible, but whether I honestly want this. Do I actually feel an inner urge, a readiness, a necessity to be as free as it has been explained by him? Am I totally committed to freedom, willing to leave all traditions, spiritual sy-

---

67 Krishnamurti (1969): 18

stems, all my knowledge and any believe in authorities behind? I guess I am not (yet). Therefore, I believe that spiritual techniques, methods and gurus function to prepare people and to create this urge, interest and determination to being free – but do not to actually set us free.

According to Dietrich, Krishnamurti is an important, ground-breaking personality in the field of Peace Studies. He had been one of the first, few, world-renowned spiritual philosophers that lived a *transrational* approach to peace. Dietrich wrote:

> Krishnamurti smashes [...] all doctrines of the western *modernity* and at the same time those of the Indian tradition. He dispossesses the saints of their superiority, refuses to offer promises of salvation or instructions for action and thereby indicates the way to the holistic approaches of *transpersonal* psychology and the *transrational* peaces.[68]

Another famous spiritual philosopher who also furthered a *transrational* approach to peaces and whose understanding of freedom is an inspiration to me, is Osho.

My interpretation of Osho's ideas of freedom

Osho was born in India in1931 and died there in 1990. Osho cannot be categorized into one specific religion, philosophy or spiritual discipline. Contrary to Krishnamurti, he did not eschew to propose methods to provide insights for individuals into themselves and the mystery of life. Osho developed various dynamic meditation practises and explained the core of ancient Eastern wisdom-traditions such as Tantra, Shivaism, Yoga, Taoism, Zen Buddhism, Sufism, Jainism and others to people in the so-called West. He was also inspired by European philosophers such as Aristotle, Plato, Heraclitus, Jean Paul Sartre and many others.[69] He knew about "*modern* philosophy and psychology, casually and frequently

68 Dietrich (2008): 338 Translated by the author.
69 Osho (2007)

quoted Nietzsche, Heidegger, Freud, Jung, Adler and Reich, and interwove his teachings with the findings, therapeutic techniques, methods and the vocabulary of *Encounter*, Psychodrama and Gestalttherapy."[70]

Osho studied philosophy in India in the 1950s, became a university professor and then a spiritual teacher to increasingly more disciples. Osho became famous to Europeans and North Americans, and he founded a commune in Pune, India, and later on in Oregon, USA. Throughout his life he has been loved, admired, praised, worshipped and at the same time harshly criticized, hated and feared. Undoubtedly, he lived a scandalous life as a master in the art of provocation who knew how to trigger shocks and popular outrage – and apart from enjoying it he also hoped to open the eyes of people. A great number of people despised him for his hedonistic life-style, for his open, shameless talks on sexuality or for certain disputable incidences which took place in the commune in Oregon. Furthermore, he was criticized for speaking out against authorities and institutions, while at the same time not hesitating to take on the role of the liberator – unlike Krishnamurti – and build up an institutionalized movement.[71] Despite their differences and although they never met each other, according to Osho he and Krishnamurti have perhaps been "the two persons closest to each other in the whole world"[72].

Today many of Osho's meditation techniques are popular in Europe, the USA, Canada and other countries. Osho was one of the leading figures to bring eastern spiritual traditions to the so-called *west* and probably the first to radically critique the alienated form of sexuality as it is practised in modern societies, which ignore its spiritual, holy dimensions. I have chosen Osho's definition of freedom because I appreciate that he dared to risk being unpopular; he spoke out straightforwardly no matter if it would bring him praise or disrepute. I have the impression that he had the courage to be himself – which is a crucial facet of freedom.

The three dimensions of freedom

My research bases on the book "freedom – The Courage to Be Yourself"[73] which was composed out of different speeches by Osho dealing with the question of

70 Dietrich (2008): 340 Translated by the author.
71 Dietrich (2008): 340 Translated by the author.
72 Osho World (1986): Death of the mystic, J. Krishnamurti, Osho's tribute
73 Osho (2004)

freedom. In the beginning of his elaborations, he divided freedom into three dimensions.

At First, there is the physical freedom which means that the "body is not enchained, not categorized as lower than anyone else's, that there is an equality as far as the body is concerned."[74] Osho mentioned slaves, women and races that are, or have for a long time been, victims to authorities who were in power over their bodies. Prisoners, who are forced to live behind iron bars and can usually only leave their cells for one hour a day, are obviously not physically free. The second dimension is psychological freedom. This implies not being "slaves of political ideologies, social ideologies, or religious ideologies."[75] Therefore psychological freedom is to be free from limiting concepts, not bound to a moral value system, not hypnotised by an ideology without the freedom to observe it critically from a certain distance. Thirdly, spiritual freedom is the ultimate freedom, "which is knowing that you are not the body, knowing that you are not the mind, knowing that you are only pure consciousness. That knowledge comes through meditation."[76]

In this chapter I focus on the second dimension of freedom for the following reasons. I research theatre work which is applied in prisons, hence I will deal with physically unfree people and I do not intend to find methods to set them physically free. Spiritual freedom is too abstract and unseizable for me at this point in life, whereas I do think it is possible for me to grasp and work with the dimension of psychological freedom. In the following pages I will explain certain facets of freedom that Osho regarded relevant.

Freedom is to be yourself

> The freedom from something is not true freedom. The freedom to do anything you want to do is also not the freedom I am talking about. My vision of freedom is to be yourself.[77]
>
> Accept the responsibility of being yourself as you are, with all that is good and with all that is bad, with all that is beautiful and that which is not beautiful. In that acceptance transcendence happens and one becomes free.[78]

74 Osho (2004): Foreword *x*
75 Osho (2004): Foreword *x*
76 Osho (2004): Foreword *xii*
77 Osho (2004): Foreword *xiv*

As the book I refer to is called "freedom – The Courage to Be Yourself", these two quotes appear crucial to me. Why is being oneself the essential aspect of freedom? As I understand Osho's quotes, being oneself implies the following. One needs to be free from outer authorities that establish norms of *how to be a decent, successful human being* and *how to behave* in society; Free from authorities who determine what is good, polite, lovely or evil, sinful, abnormal; Free from experts who decide whether something is possible or impossible, whether somebody is a success or a failure.

It is certainly a daring act to free oneself from these forces who rear individuals into well-educated puppets with good manners and a lot of knowledge, but who have lost their spontaneity and courage to rebel. It takes courage to step out of a system where the expectations of others dictate a large part of who we are. In order to get a glimpse of who I am, I need to reconnect to my own feelings, needs and perceptions – emotionally and also physically. Obviously, everyone who is not connected to their own body is an easy prey to experts who seem to know better than we do ourselves. (Then, our body's appetite does not dictate what we should eat, instead a nutritionist does or we do not know how to stay healthy and depend on doctors to sell us a cure.)

From my point of view, Osho proposes to get rid of all conditionings and instead look inward to become aware of what we feel in any moment and then act out of this insight. It takes courage to be oneself, because knowing what we truly feel, need and want enables us to determinedly strive for it, which will not always be comfortable or understandable to our environment. Additionally, it will be a challenge for oneself, because being authentic might cause the feeling of being different to others. One might temporarily lose orientation because suddenly the concepts that one's environment takes for granted do not feel true anymore. Hence, living authentically means to have the courage to take a stand for all my actions, my opinions, my feelings – even though they might disappoint others – and this is certainly less convenient than swimming in the safe dullness of the masses. Practising authenticity is a long-term process and takes patience, because many of us were educated to be polite and fit in rather than to speak our minds straightforwardly.

78 Osho (2004): 2

Freedom is responsibility

> You think not being responsible makes you free? Not feeling responsible for your actions, for your thoughts, for your being, do you think you are freed from all the consequences?[79]

> This is my experience: the day I took complete responsibility for myself, I found the doors of freedom opening to me. They go together.[80]

In these statements Osho highlights that responsibility goes together with daring to be oneself. For example, imagine somebody is enthusiastically curious about having a certain experience, yet she knows that by doing so, a person who is close to her would be hurt. Nevertheless, she prefers to have this experience, to cross the boundaries of the known, to try out something new – and thereby takes the risk of hurting this person. I personally understand responsibility, as a confidence in which there is no higher court that can judge me, than I myself. I am the one who will repent or enjoy the consequences, yet I can never escape them. I would suffer to see a person hurt and would understand that my action or inaction leading to that hurt had totally been my decision. As freedom is responsibility, you are the only instance to judge yourself; no moral value system, no God, no law – but it is you who is in charge of your thoughts, deeds and their consequences.

Furthermore Osho emphasizes to take responsibility for everything that I find good and everything that I see as bad. If I lie, I must admit honestly to myself that I lied. Nobody forced me – it was my choice not to be honest. Responsibility in this approach goes together with an attitude of radical honesty towards oneself and others, about everything one feels, thinks and does. He realizes that he is not a victim, but instead, he has his life in his hands.

---

79 Osho (2004): 29
80 Osho (2004): 31

Freedom is understanding and consciousness

> Freedom means understanding. One has understood the game, and seeing that this is the way that the soul is prevented from growing, the way one is not allowed to be oneself, one simply gets out of it with no scar on the soul. One forgives and forgets and remains without any clinging to the society in the name of love or in the name of hate.[81]

Freedom starts at the moment when somebody realizes that she does not want to keep on playing this game and decides to experience something else, something beyond the boundaries that condition her. Freedom, in my interpretation of Osho, is a simple *getting out* and *letting go* of restrictive, narrowing (self-)condition(ing)s without wasting energy by fighting against them; Simply turning completely towards conditions in which one feels freer.

Freedom is an opportunity

> Freedom only provides an opportunity for you; it is not the goal itself.[82]

> Freedom is simply an opportunity to find a definition for yourself, a true, authentic individuality, and the joy in making the world around you a little better and more beautiful – add a few more roses, a little more greenery, a few more oases.[83]

These quotes have opened my eyes to new questions. Why dream of freedom *only*? What do I want to do with this freedom? What do I do when I have reached it? It is probably useless to strive for freedom as an ultimate goal without having a clear vision of what one's *free life* could look like. This is also relevant within my discourse about freedom inside of a prison. Here, freedom would mean not to stop one's imagination at the point where a prisoner leaves the jail, but to start at this point by creating an image of what a free life could be.

---

81 Osho (2004): 49
82 Osho (2004): 114
83 Osho (2004): 116

Freedom is creativity

> Independence in itself does not mean much. Just by being independent you will not be fulfilled. It is good to be out of the prison, but for what? Independence for what? Freedom for what? Remember freedom has two aspects: first, freedom from, and second freedom for. [...] Many people only attain the first kind of freedom, freedom from – free from the parents, free from the church, free from the organisation, free from this and that, free from all kinds of prisons. But for what? [...]
>
> The positive has to be known – freedom to create, freedom to be, freedom to express, to sing your song, to dance your dance. That is the third stage: creativity.[84]

Osho highlights that freedom goes beyond an attitude of rejection. However, rejection is necessary if it causes an intense questioning of seemingly natural circumstances. Authorities, oppressive systems and established truths must become visible as factors that manipulate people and rip them from their self-determination. They ought to be deconstructed. Yet, this is not everything.

Apart from rejection, people would have to reconnect to their own bodies, feelings, and their own truths. Creativity gives me the potential to express what I am or to imagine what I could be, to express what the world is like or to materialize a vision of how it could be. Creativity is a proactive interaction with one's surrounding, rooting in interconnectedness and flourishing into unknown fields. Freedom for "will give you wings. Freedom from, at the most, can take away your handcuffs."[85] This argument explains why I, in this thesis, focus on the creative potential of Theatre of the Oppressed in prisons rather than critiquing the existence of prisons – which I also regard necessary.

Summary of Osho's perspective on freedom

Concerning Osho's understanding of psychological freedom, the essential facet of freedom is the courage to be oneself. Daring to be oneself requires the courage to take responsibility for being a certain way, as well as for every single thought, every action and all their consequences. Freedom for Osho is freedom *for* self-responsibility, *for* creating one's life or the world in a way that one deems beauti-

84 Osho (2004): 52
85 Osho (2004): 87

ful, *for* a joyful celebration of life's mystery. Freedom is an opportunity, but not the goal in itself.

As a next step all previously elaborated perspectives on freedom will be compared and scrutinized for the contradictions and communalities between them.

COMPARING FOUR PERSPECTIVES ON FREEDOM

I will now highlight contradictions and communalities between the four perspectives on freedom introduced in the previous sub-chapters. Firstly, my personal perspective on freedom; Secondly, the etymological notion of the term *Freiheit*, freedom, in the German language, throughout the ages; Thirdly, the freedom understanding of Jiddu Krishnamurti and lastly Osho's perspective on freedom. They will be compared, discussed and related to each other.

I will start out with contradictions and continue with their communalities. Subsequently I filter out those facets of freedom which might be of value in the context of Theatre of the Oppressed in prisons. Accordingly, a definition evolves which forms the basis for my research. From then on I will continue working with this definition, evaluating in which sense the application of Theatre of the Oppressed in prisons changes the sensation of inner freedom for the inmates.

Contradictions

Freedom from or freedom for?

The first, very fundamental contradiction is the question of whether one understands freedom mainly as freedom *from* or as freedom *for/to*, which is a differentiation that Osho often highlighted. Krishnamurti, in my opinion, focuses on the freedom *from*. Freedom from inner and outer authorities, concepts, conditionings, prejudices, attachments and being free from judging – these are a few examples for what he describes as freedom. This difference is apparent in the titles of their books. Krishnamurti's book is called "Freedom *from* the known", whereas Osho's is titled "freedom- The Courage *to* Be Yourself."

The focus of Krishnamurti explains why I have often had the impression that reading his words radically cleans up my brain. Rigid concepts undergo deconstruction, useless ballast is disposed, outmoded believes are dusted off, the pillars of securities in which I believe(d) were heavily jolted. His statements sorted waste in my mind and afterwards, I often felt a bit fresher, emptier – yet also confused, insecure or frustrated. Being taught self-responsibility by Krishnamurti, I wondered why I should want this empty, fresh, *free* room if there is no *beauty* and *connection* in it. He never mentioned *trust*, which is a crucial aspect of freedom for me.

After having the rug pulled from under my feet I came across a quote of Osho saying “Krishnamurti’s teaching is beautiful, but too serious. Life needs a little playfulness, a little humor, a little laughter.”[86] The fundamental contradiction between the two becomes apparent in the following statement of Osho about Krishnamurti.

> Only on that point am I in absolute disagreement with him; otherwise, he was a genius. He has penetrated as deeply as possible into every dimension of man’s spirituality, but it is all like a desert, tiring. I would like you back in the garden of Eden, innocent, not serious, but like small children playing. This whole existence is playful. This whole existence is full of humor; you just need the sense of humor and you will be surprised…. Existence is hilarious. Everything is in a dancing mood, you just have to be in the same mood to understand it.[87]

Osho favours the freedom *to* be oneself, freedom *for* having joy, dancing, celebrating – being free for creativity! He praised the beauty of life and the potential for consciousness that lies in sensuality.

Working with Theatre of the Oppressed in prisons, both aspects of freedom are important: Jolting structures which appear as natural but are in fact oppressive – as the prison system – while on the other hand creating ways of perceiving oneself as creative, intelligent being with an incredible, inward potential. Freedom *from* and freedom *for* – or in my own terms *critical thinking* and *trusting* – both go hand in hand such as destruction and creation.

Freedom as exclusive privilege or as uniting force?

Concerning the etymological notion of freedom there is one outstanding contradiction with all other perspectives. The term *Freiheit*, freedom, in former times,

86 Osho World (1986): Death of the mystic, J. Krishnamurti, Osho’s tribute
87 Osho World (1986): Death of the mystic, J. Krishnamurti, Osho’s tribute

often meant that those belonging to one's kin, one's family, one's dear and beloved ones owned the privilege of freedom. Contrarily, the understanding of freedom from Krishnamurti and Osho goes into a different direction: There shall no longer be a judgemental "we" and "the others", because this separation emerged out of conditionings, out of the known, out of prejudices and projections which are the opposite of a spontaneous, fresh, free mind.

Freiheit in this context means to be free from sticking to concepts that fix people to certain characteristics producing borderlines which makes connection impossible. My personal perspective emphasises the importance of trust in the humanity of the other regardless of belonging to a certain kin, status in society, nationality or other illusory lines of separation.

Freedom as individual experience or together with others?

Interestingly, the understanding of freedom between the etymological notion and the joint understanding of Osho, Krishnamurti and I conflict on which different entities experience freedom. The etymological notion sees freedom, *Freiheit*, as a kind of group-experience. A group belongs together, they are dear to each other, care for one another, protect and love each other. Freeing someone, *jemanden freien*, also meant to court and want to marry a person. Consequently, freedom is bound to bonds of affection and relationship, and therefore not experienced by one single person individually.

Osho, Krishnamurti and I described freedom as an individual sensation. If an individual is free from certain conditions and if she is free to be creative – this is freedom. Free individuals can meet and relate to each other, but the sensation of freedom, does not depend on other people but could be experienced, for example, in nature. This contradiction is certainly embedded in the context of our age, the 20th and 21st century, in which individuality and independence became increasingly more important values.

Communalities

Free neck as an image for self-responsibility

There is one aspect of the etymological notion that I approve, which is the fact that the term *Freiheit* originates from the image of the *freihals*, a person who has a free neck. I understand *free neck* not only as a sign for physical freedom, in the sense of being in power over one's own body, but also as psychological freedom implying that one is one's own master and disciple at the same time and hence in power over her own thoughts and actions. In freedom there is no authority to either physically decapitate, or psychologically *de-mind* a person. Having a free neck goes together with self-responsibility that none can take away.

Freedom from authorities and thereby experiencing for oneself

Krishnamurti and Osho highlighted that freedom is the courage to experience for oneself. Scrutinizing the dependency on authorities is the precondition to find out what is true for me and what I have been taught but now I question. This aspect of freedom, the freedom to find out the truth for oneself without anyone telling you, is significant in the worldview of Theatre of the Oppressed. In any Theatre of the Oppressed forum play[88] it has to be a common denominator that all participants first collect their own experiences, act them out and then create a space where everyone tries out his or her own imagined solution. There is none to teach a prescriptive method of solving a conflict or tackling an issue.

Freedom aspects that I take for evaluating the application of Theatre of the Oppressed in prison

The essential facets of freedom that I keep after the comparison of all four perspectives are:
Taking *responsibility* for oneself, the group and the society one lives in.
Trust in oneself, others and life.
Critical thinking, in the sense of becoming aware of oppressive situations and discriminating structures; Realizing that most of the time there is not a single person to blame for becoming a criminal or ending up in prison, but that there is a whole system that contributes to one's way into criminality and determines the characteristics of *the usual suspect*, which is then easily found.
Self-confidence and being aware of one's own value, daring to be oneself.
Trying something new and thereby becoming aware, or *free of one's conditionings* and behaviour patterns which keep one from acting spontaneously in a new situation.
Spontaneous, unprejudiced perception
Being present in the sense of being aware of what happens in the very moment in oneself, in one's body, in the group, in the process.

---

88 On page 72 the method of Forum Theatre will be explained further.

Not relying more on any outer authority than on one's own experiences. Theatre of the Oppressed works with the common knowledge and experiences of a group and does not put the responsibility for change to so-called experts, politicians, artists.

Conclusion

These aspects will be the criteria for determining whether a process of Theatre of the Oppressed actually transforms the sensation of 'inner freedom' for the prison inmates.

Inner freedom is to have the opportunity to create, to try out new ways and to have individualistic experience. Inner freedom is the courage to be oneself and to take responsibility for what one thinks and does. Inner freedom is a balance between trust and critical thinking.

The last and very essential aspect is that *Freedom is not the goal itself, it is an opportunity to create*. This has been one of the most inspiring arguments of Osho for me. Freedom in this sense is an unburdened, carefree, spontaneous state out of which *everything* can emerge.

> Freedom in itself has no meaning, unless it is freedom for something, something creative – freedom to sculpt, freedom to dance, freedom to create music, poetry, painting. Unless you turn your freedom into a creative realization, you will feel sad.[89]

With this quote I want to conclude the chapter on freedom and introduce the following chapter which deals with Theatre of the Oppressed. As the quote highlighted that "unless you turn your freedom into a creative realization, you will feel sad", I know that for me it is of little satisfaction to merely feel free *from...* without creating something that makes sense and brings joy. This is where the topics freedom and Theatre of the Oppressed overlap, within me: Being free to work creatively, to make theatre, to act, to post questions, to criticize and to transform structures.

---

89 Osho (2004): 113

THEATRE OF THE OPPRESSED

Introduction

This chapter gives an overview on theory and praxis of Theatre of the Oppressed. It is divided into a theoretical part in which the beginning and ongoing development of Theatre of the Oppressed is explained and a practical part which describes various theatrical methods. I will start out with the origin of Theatre of the Oppressed in the late 1960's and early 1970's and connect it to the biography of Augusto Boal, its creator. Subsequently certain theatrical, pedagogical and philosophical figures and theories that influenced Boal and his form of theatre are introduced. These sources of inspiration, especially Paolo Freire, contributed to certain principles of Theatre of the Oppressed. After depicting those principles, we enter the practical part of this chapter, starting with a presentation of the greater, most popular methods. Then, a quick idea of how Theatre of the Oppressed is applied today will be given. For more in-depth details I recommend looking at the well elaborated homepage of Theatre of the Oppressed.[90] Finally, I will mention critical viewpoints on Theatre of the Oppressed originating from my personal perspective, literature research and practical experiences.

THE BEGINNING OF THEATRE OF THE OPPRESSED

> His [Augusto Boal's] now classic text *Theatre of the Oppressed*, written when the repressive political climate of Brazil in the late 1960s and early 1970s had forced him into exile, could be considered essential reading for anyone engaged with the question whether theatre might be able to effect transformation in people's lives.[91]

This quote introduces Augusto Boal with one of the major aims of his lifework: The creation of a form of theatre, which has the potential to transform people's

---

90 www.theatreoftheoppressed.org The homepage gives an overview over innumerable projects in various countries, provides literature and offers contact addresses.

91 Babbage (2004): 1

lives. In 1971 Boal created Newspaper Theatre, which was the first method in the arsenal of Theatre of the Oppressed. For almost 40 years, new methods, games and theatre techniques have been developed and added to the Theatre of the Oppressed. All of them aim at raising consciousness about different kinds of oppression and gradually liberating from it. From its beginning until now Theatre of the Oppressed understood itself as democratic and humanistic[92] theatre. Furthermore it is often categorized as political, radical and participative.

Augusto Boal has put enormous commitment into collecting, creating and integrating a great number of games and techniques into the framework of Theatre of the Oppressed. He hardly paused to spread those methods and their inherent messages all over the globe. However, fascinated by his charisma and popularity one easily falls into the trap of reducing Theatre of the Oppressed to him only, ignoring the contribution of a world-wide network of practitioners, jokers, participants, *spect-actors*, critics, opponents, authors, people who posed questions and many others. Because it cannot be denied that Theatre of the Oppressed currently circulates around Boal as person, founder, workshop leader and author, I will elaborate on embedding the Theatre of the Oppressed as we know it today, into the context of his life.

Biography of Augusto Boal

Augusto Boal was born in 1931 in Rio de Janeiro and grew up when Brazil was under dictatorship. His parents had migrated from Portugal to Brazil and were economically comfortable enough to afford a solid education for Augusto. His love for theatre revealed itself in his early years.[93] Although he studied Chemistry, partly in order to please his father, he never gave up his passion for theatre. His studies of Theatre in the United States fruitfully inspired his subsequent engagement as a director of theatre plays in Sao Paolo's *Teatro de Arena*, from 1956 to 1971. The *Arena* theatre also had a studio affiliated with dramatists and actors in which plays were written in collective cooperation.[94] During that time Boal frequently worked with unions, groups of students or farmers and thereby gradually approached those sectors of society where oppression became an un-

92 Theatre of the Oppressed: Declaration of Principles
93 Boal (2001): 75f
94 Ried (2007): 9

deniably obvious issue. The military coups in 1964 and 1968 lead to a period of severe repression which strongly affected their theatrical work.[95]

> All forms of cultural expression came in for heavy censorship. However, while this period saw the arts under attack, it also witnessed the rise of a theatre actively opposed to the dictatorship in the work of such groups as Arena and Teatro Ofícina, both based in Sao Paolo, and Opinião, based in Rio de Janeiro.[96]

Due to the suppression of critical arts by the military dictatorship, Augusto Boal and others were imprisoned, tortured and forced into exile. In exile, Boal collected and developed a range of theatre practises and games, which he subsumed as *Theatre of the Oppressed.* Inspired by Paolo Freire, with whom he shared the approach, that there can only be sustainable emancipation and social change if the people are not excluded from bringing about these changes, he decided to contribute to alphabetisation courses in Peru. At that time in Brazil, the right to vote had been tied to the ability to read and write.[97] Therefore, Boal and Freire rendered that the ability to read would bring about the capability to participate in political decision-making.

Augusto Boal lived in Argentinean exile from which he moved to Portugal and then to France in 1978. In 1979 a centre dedicated to the development and dissemination of Theatre of the Oppressed, CEDITADE[98], had been founded in Paris with Boal as its art director. Its goals were to scrutinize the Theatre of the Oppressed techniques in theory and practise, develop them further and apply them to the cultural and social sector in France.[99] During that time Boal and the members of CEDITADE began raising the issue of psychological oppression and as a consequence developed *The Rainbow of Desire*. It ought to be said that his wife Cecilia Boal certainly inspired and contributed to this development. She has been a psychotherapist and worked together with Boal, yet unfortunately she is rarely mentioned in literature about Augusto and it is difficult to find out more about who she is.

In 1986 Augusto and his family returned to Brazil where he, together with his colleagues, established a permanent Centre for Theatre of the Oppressed (CTO) in Rio de Janeiro. In 1992 Boal was appointed to become a *vereador*, member of

95 Babbage (2004): 3-9
96 Babbage (2004): 3
97 Ried (2007): 37
98 "Centre d'étude et de diffusion des techniques actives d'expression (Méthodes Boal)"
99 Frey (1989): 18

the council, of the Brazilian government in the sector of arts and culture in Rio de Janeiro. During that time they developed the *Legislative Theatre* which aimed at a democratisation of politics and laws.

Since then, Augusto Boal has published "The Aesthetics of the Oppressed"[100], worked on Theatre of the Oppressed prison projects in Brazil, travelled the world facilitating workshops and was involved in many other activities.

Augusto Boal's death

On May 2nd in 2009 the sad message of Augusto Boal's death went through the news. At the age of 78 he died in Brazil. "'Come closer he would say. Come closer.' Now he is further away than ever — and yet we may feel closer than ever to him. The greatest Joker has left the stage."[101] With these words Adrian Jackson, translator of Boal's books, practitioner, founder of *cardboard citizens*[102], and friend of Boal expressed his condolence.

Paul Heritage says about Boal "His work is valuable because it is utilitarian, but it is loved because it promises a heroic vision of what theatre could achieve."[103] This quote reflects that Boal's creation of theatre is promising, heroic, visionary and most important: It is loved!

I personally consider that the charismatic personality of Augusto Boal and his love for what he was doing accounted greatly for its success. I met Boal twice, once in a workshop and again at a conference. I was touched by his humour, his mimics and gestures, the sparks in his eyes when he spoke, the enthusiasm for his work and his love for life and human beings. This is how I perceived his presence. Theatre of the Oppressed methods are practised on every continent; thousands of people have already enjoyed its games. I think it is impossible to deny that Boal's charisma certainly had an enormous impact on how Theatre of the Oppressed messages were received and spread. This spreading, however, would have never been possible without innumerable committed practitioners.

Now, that Augusto Boal has physically left the *stage*, the international community of Theatre of the Oppressed is apparently moving even closer together, driven by the question of how to continue Boal's vision – which is now no longer his, but the vision of so many! Now, as the one *master* has handed over his

---

100 Boal (2006)
101 Theatre of the Oppressed (2009)
102 See http://www.cardboardcitizens.org.uk/
103 Heritage in Babbage (2004): 33

responsibilities to a community, a great number of people cooperate to create the future of Theatre of the Oppressed. *The show must go on* – and I am confident it will.

I was in the process of completing this book, when I received the message of Augusto Boal's death. Hence, in every chapter that deals with Augusto Boal, except this one, I had already written about him in the present. I wondered whether I would better *actualize* all chapters by replacing sentences such as "Augusto Boal *is*..." to "Augusto Boal *was*..." however, this did not feel right. I decided to leave them the way they are because both are true: Boal has physically left this world, while at the same time he and his vision are present and vividly alive!

PHILOSOPHICAL BACKGROUND

Theatrical Sources of Inspiration

Augusto Boal has been influenced greatly by two theatre makers: Bertold Brecht[104] and Konstantin Sergejev Stanislawsky[105]. Boal adopted Brecht's assumption that society can transform through the means of theatre. In contrast to Brecht, Boal calls for going beyond mere reflection and emphasises the importance of taking action.[106]

One further important source of inspiration was Jakob Levy Moreno[107]. Moreno has been a psychologist who found in theatre – especially in *Stegreiftheater* which is a form of theatre based on spontaneous improvisation with minimal preparation – a possibility to cope with personal and social conflicts.[108] In the 1920s Moreno developed *Psychodrama* in Vienna, Austria. Central techniques of Psychodrama such as duplication, mirroring and swapping roles are essential in Theatre of the Oppressed as well.[109] The main discrepancy between these two approaches is that Psychodrama aims at the therapeutical healing of the individual within society, whereas Theatre of the Oppressed emphasises the political transformation of society.

---

104 1898-1956
105 1863-1938
106 Ried (2007): 91
107 1889-1974
108 Ried (2007): 50f
109 Ried (2007): 91

Boal was interested in theatre forms from various authors, geographical regions and styles. In his studies of theatre in New York in the early 1950s "Boal engaged with work by virtually all major modern European and American dramatists , as well as with Shakespeare and the Greeks, and the broad dramatic 'movements' of realism, symbolism, surrealism and expressionism."[110]

> There are overlaps with Brecht's Epic Theatre, with 'happenings' and the Depression-era Living Newspaper in the US, and with the Psychodrama of Jacob Moreno. Boal's thinking is broadly informed by classical Greek drama, by Shakespeare, Stanislavsky, Marx and Freud, among others.[111]

Pedagogical and Philosophical Sources of Inspiration

The term "Theatre of the Oppressed" expresses its connection to "Pedagogy of the Oppressed", by Paulo Freire[112], who has been an influential Brazilian pedagogue from the 1960s up to now. Freire's theoretical works are internationally known and due to his practical commitment to alphabetisation his methods were applied in 1967 to all state-run alphabetisation programs.[113]

Paulo Freire's approach to education became an essential component of the idea of Theatre of the Oppressed: None should teach with an attitude of superiority and authority due to his profession to teach knowledge. Rather, one ought to perceive oneself as teacher-student or student-teacher, whereas students learn from their teacher while at the same time, the teacher is learning from her students. In this understanding of education, both learn from each other in a mutual dialogue. Paolo Freire criticized the traditional form of education, which he termed the *banking system*.

> This is the 'banking' concept of education, in which the scope of action allowed to the students extends only as far as receiving, filing and storing of deposits. They [...] become collectors or cataloguers of the things they store. But in the last analysis, it is the people themselves who are filed away through lack of creativity, transformation, and knowledge in this misguided system.[114]

110 Babbage (2004): 7
111 Babbage (2004): 32
112 1921-1997
113 Ried (2007): 37
114 Freire (1996): 53

Augusto Boal implemented this pedagogical approach to his theatre practises and criticized the passivity of spectators in theatre who, in his opinion, should better become *spect-actors*. Boal calls for an audience consisting of *spect-actors*, who actively involve themselves in a process of critical, creative and mutually inspiring interventions.

Furthermore, Paulo Freire coined the expression *conscientização*, which "refers to learning to perceive social, political and economic contradictions, and to take action against the oppressive elements of reality."[115] Augusto Boal shares this conviction of the importance to raise critical awareness about the reality one lives in, and has therefore created theatre methods which aim at more consciousness about external and internal processes.

Paulo Freire himself has been influenced by Ivan Illich, Erich Fromm, Paul Goodman[116], the co-founder of *Gestalttherapy* together with Laura and Fritz Perls, and others.[117] Both Freire and Boal often refer to Marx, whose ideological influence on them becomes apparent throughout their books. Other important sources of inspiration for Boal, from the fields of psychotherapy and philosophy, have been Wilhelm Reich[118], Sigmund Freud[119], Friedrich Nietzsche[120] and Jean Jacques Rousseau[121].[122]

Principles of Theatre of the Oppressed

Becoming Conscious of Oppression

"Any situation in which 'A' objectively exploits 'B' or hinders his or her pursuit of self-affirmation as a responsible person is one of oppression."[123] This is Paolo Freire's definition of oppression. The Theatre of the Oppressed builds up on that idea and proposes practical tools to become aware of situations in which one is

115 Freire (1996): 17
116 "[…] Anarchist peace activist and writer [...and] initiator of the Anti-Vietnam-War Movement" according to Dietrich (2008): 379 Translated by the author.
117 Ried (2007): 15
118 1897-1957
119 1856-1939
120 1844-1900
121 1712-1778
122 Ried (2007): 19
123 Freire (1996): 37

oppressed, be it by oneself, one's environment, or by political and social structures.

Oppression is very often internalized, individualised or too subtle to be perceived. Consequently, "the criteria for suppression can not only be a subjective sensation"[124], but must scrutinize the structures it is embedded in, as Julian Boal, son of Augusto Boal and an experienced theatre practitioner, highlighted.

Hence, the first step is to raise consciousness about one's own or collective oppression. The second step could be to create a space in one's head for the possibility that every seemingly hopeless situation almost always carries intrinsic alternatives in it. Therefore, several Theatre of the Oppressed methods work with this procedure: First, images are created which show one's experience of oppression, secondly an alternative image which pictures an ideal situation is sculptured and thirdly the transition from the first to the second is acted out.

Peace, not Passivity[125]

> 'Is the fundamental relationship between an actor and an audience an equal and active one, or is it a situation that encourages passivity and division?' This is the question at the heart of Augusto Boal's revolutionary Theatre of the Oppressed, originally published in 1979.[126]

With this question Boal created the *spect-actor*, an actively interacting person from the audience who jumps into the role of the protagonist whenever he or she has a proposal for an alternative way to solve a certain conflictive situation. The intention of freeing oneself from passivity first, by stepping into an active role on the stage, and then in real life moving from (political) apathy towards active participation, is especially visible in Forum Theatre. The slogan "peace not passivity" implies that Theatre of the Oppressed is about transforming existent conflicts instead of simulating a fake harmony. It is about the courage to bring up hot issues and pose critique instead of favouring passive acceptance. Or, as I would express it: Activists are more likely than *passivists* to be genuine pacifists.

124 Boal, Julian at a workshop in the ministry of Justice, Vienna, in April 2008.
125 Boal (2004)
126 Theatre of the Oppressed (2008): Books & Links – Theatre of the Oppressed

Dialogue

> The *oppressed* are those individuals or groups who are socially, culturally, politically, economically, racially, sexually, or in any other way deprived of their right to *dialogue* or in any way impaired to exercise this right.
>
> *Dialogue* is defined as to freely exchange with others, as a person and as a group, to participate in human society as equal, to respect differences and to be respected.[127]

Dialogue is possibly the foundation of the approaches of Paolo Freire and Augusto Boal. Sharing knowledge with each other; learning with and from one another; communicating one's thoughts, needs, fears and ideas to each other; escaping isolation through the insight that what appears as individual oppression is actually deeply rooted in certain social structures which affect others as well. Dialogue is a possible key to implement this. Dialogue enables people to share their thoughts and thereby enrich each other with proposals of ways to become free from oppression – this process of mutual thought-provocation is realized for example in the *Forum Theatre*. Dialogue furthermore implies to listen to one another and thereby support others in their struggles to make themselves heard.

Solidarity

> The oppressor is solidary with the oppressed only when he stops regarding the oppressed as an abstract category and sees them as persons who have been unjustly dealt with, deprived of their voice, cheated in the sale of their labor – when he stops making pious, sentimental and individualistic gestures and risks an act of love.[128]

The last words of Freire are especially interesting to me. I interpret his statement as a call for an inner, authentic attitude of solidarity which originates from *love* and the perception of the oppressed as human beings with certain needs – in place of sentimental, pitiful gestures. Solidarity, I suppose, emerges with the insight that there is no individual oppression, which would not root in one's soci-

---

127 Theatre of the Oppressed (2008): Declaration of Principles
128 Freire (1996): 32

al context. Theatre of the Oppressed continually emphasizes the importance of solidarity with the globally oppressed.

Connection

"Ultimately what Boal wants his theatre practise to do is: dissolve barriers to true connection."[129] This statement expresses the essence of my motivation for this research. There is hardly anything, which I imagine to be more beautiful and sustainably peaceful than if we, human beings, realize our true connection with each other and the nature. The insight that we are all connected – no matter whether we are oppressors in one situation and oppressed in another situation – brings about the realisation that with every act of oppression or violence, which I set is actually harmful to myself. Consequently, it is in *my own* interest to become increasingly more aware of any unconscious oppression – whether I enact it onto myself or on others.

Connection, as I imagine that it is understood from a Theatre of the Oppressed viewpoint implies the following: Gaps between parallel realities or opposing perspectives are brought into connection. The realization of the interrelatedness between poles such as wealth and poverty or power and oppression might enhance an urge to act. Being aware of these connections makes it difficult to escape our responsibility for what happens in the world.

Everybody is creative

The philosophy of Augusto Boal is the assumption that everyone is creative and everyone is an actor. Creativity must not be left to the artists! Neither shall politics be left to the politicians, nor education to the educators! None shall give away these aspects of an active life in order to leave them to so-called experts, as this is a form of incapacitating oneself. Consequently, in Boal's concept of theatre there are no passive spectators. Everybody is invited to act. The formerly passive spectators turn into active *spect-actors*.

129 Bettencourt (2000)

PRAXIS OF THEATRE OF THE OPPRESSED

> It is only when the oppressed find the oppressor out and become involved in the organized struggle for their liberation that they begin to believe in themselves. This discovery cannot be purely intellectual, but must involve action; nor can it be limited to mere activism, but must include serious reflection: only then it will be a praxis.[130]

With this quote Freire formulates the fundament for what Boal continues in his theatre praxis: The combination of reflection and action. As mentioned before, many Theatre of the Oppressed techniques set out with reflection on the circumstances as they are in the present and continue with action aimed at a construction of freer circumstances. In the following, Boal's praxis, put into practise through the six major methods of Theatre of the Oppressed will be explained along the structure of the *Tree of the Theatre of the Oppressed.*

130 Freire (1996): 47

Tree of the Theatre of the Oppressed

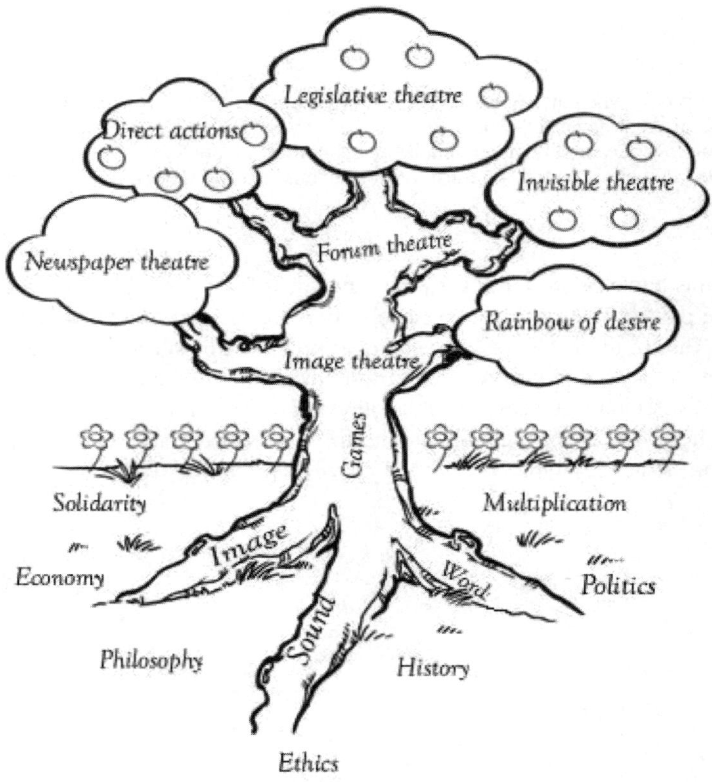

Boal (2004): Theatre of the Oppressed

Methods of Theatre of the Oppressed

"Theatre of the Oppressed was born in 1971, in Brazil"[131], as Augusto Boal defines its starting point. Since then methods, games and theatre techniques have been developed which all aim at raising consciousness about oppression and the

131 Boal (2004)

liberation from it. The transformation from a passive member of society to one who actively participates, criticizes and creates is a crucial objective within the Theatre of the Oppressed.

To realize these ideas "Boal identified stages by which the spectator – in his view fundamentally a passive being – could become an actor. The proposed steps are as follows: (1) knowing the body; (2) making the body expressive; (3) the theatre as language; and (4) the theatre as discourse."[132] Getting to know one's body, sensitising one's senses and making the body expressive is cultivated especially through various games. I do not go deeper into games furthering body awareness even though I regard them as fundamentally important. I will rather explain the six major methods of Theatre of the Oppressed, in which I perceive a strong orientation towards point (3) and (4), theatre as language and theatre as discourse. These methods mainly aim at expressing thoughts, critique, feelings, desires or function to spark self-reflection and debates about critical issues.

The following exemplification of Theatre of the Oppressed methods will be arranged according to the picture of the Theatre of the Oppressed tree. Hence, I will explain the methods not in a chronological way, according to the years of their invention, but rather along the structure of the tree starting out with Image Theatre, continuing with Newspaper Theatre, Rainbow of Desire, Forum Theatre, Invisible Theatre and closing with Legislative Theatre.

Image Theatre

Image Theatre is the fundament of various other Theatre of the Oppressed methods. Initially it was elaborated with the intention to "establish dialogue among Indigenous Nations and Spanish descendants, in Colombia, Venezuela, Mexico"[133]. Up to now it holds the objective to facilitate dialogue.

The practise starts out with someone proposing a theme – as for example *oppression*. Then the participants form groups and every person silently creates statues which personally express that theme. These images reflect their individually perceived reality and are discussed afterwards. The task can then be to imagine an ideal image, as for example one which illustrates 'freedom from oppression'. This image is then arranged by forming statues of the participants. Now the question is: How can one get from the first image to the *ideal* image? In our example

132 Babbage (2004): 20; Boal (1989): 46f
133 Boal (2004)

the question would be: Which is the action that ought to be taken to get free from a certain oppressive situation? Based on this question a third image is created which pictures the transition from the first, unfree condition to the desired alternative state. Through these three stages a static image is developed into a dynamic scene.[134]

Forum Theatre, Rainbow of Desire and other methods often start out with that process described above, because it helps to identify crucial issues and enhances the discussion around themes that might then be elaborated further.

Newspaper Theatre

Newspaper Theatre was the first method of Theatre of the Oppressed and was developed during an era of military dictatorship. It originally aimed at dealing with local problems, but was soon spread all over Brazil.[135] Newspaper Theatre offers 11 different ways of reading from a newspaper. These methods "are devised to help anyone to make a theatrical scene using a piece of news from a newspaper, or from any other written material, like reports of a political meeting, texts from the Bible, from the Constitution of a country, the Declaration of Human Rights."[136] The printed material is usually combined with further elements such as pantomimic demonstration of the content, the addition of unpleasant facts to make the picture more complete, or a rhythm, which gives a different connotation to the content.

Newspaper Theatre aims at raising critical awareness about the seeming neutrality of media. It can also highlight shocking, annoying or unsettling headlines by reading them out aloud. Furthermore it might add background information and contextual facts to an article, which displays reality in a simplistic or manipulative way.

From the eleven given techniques I would like to outline the *crossed reading*, which I myself practised in a Theatre of the Oppressed Workshop.[137] Through the *crossed reading*[138] a confrontation of different perspectives is created. We collected headlines that reported on worldwide starvation-statistics and contra-

134 Boal (1989): 241
135 Boal (2004)
136 Boal (2004)
137 In January 2009, Vienna, with Birgit Fritz in the framework of a seven-months training course in methods of Augusto Boal.
138 Boal (1979): 143, "Crossed reading: two items are read in crossed (alternating) form, one throwing light on the other, explaining it, giving it a new dimension."

sted them with a headline, saying that every third dog in Austria is obese. We took a quote about the lack of access to drinking water in different African countries on the one hand and added an advertisement for a five star cruise ship which promoted its several swimming pools, cruising along the Eastern African coast. We selected a report on people who fled hunger and opposed it with a diet proposal, designed to get rid of some additional Christmas holiday pounds. Out of the chosen headlines we created a rap-song and performed it in public.

Confronting these headlines, which report on totally different life-realities, opened our eyes to the connection between those perverted extremes while at the same time expressing our critique against the global gap between wealth and poverty. Newspaper Theatre aims to raise awareness and to provoke a critical examination of newspapers and headlines that claim to picture *reality*.

The Rainbow of Desire

This method was developed by Augusto Boal and his theatre group in Paris in the late 1980's. Realizing that the oppression he faced in Brazil varied greatly from the oppressions experienced by most Europeans, Boal elaborated on 'prospective', 'introspective' and 'extraversion' techniques which mainly dealt with internalized oppression and subsumed them in his book "The Rainbow of Desire – The Boal Method of Theatre and Therapy"[139]

> For someone like me, fleeing explicit dictatorship of a cruel and brutal nature, it was natural that these themes should at first seem superficial and scarcely worthy of attention. It was as if I was always asking, mechanically: 'But where are the cops?' Because I was used to working with concrete, visible oppressions.[140]

"Recognition that these internalised oppressions could impact severely on individual freedom – for example leading to depression, physical illness or suicide – persuaded Boal of their importance"[141], Babbage explained.

I appreciate his shift of perspective towards the oppression that takes place inside of us – the process by which we become our own oppressors. In "The Rainbow of Desire" Boal broached the issues of resignation, fear and social masks

139 Boal (1998)
140 Boal (1998): 8
141 Babbage (2004): 23

behind which we tend to hide ourselves. He furthermore developed the concept of 'cops in the head'. He defined the 'cop' as "the image present in our heads, at a point of action, which obliges us to do what we don't want to do or prevents us from doing what we do want to do."[142]

I personally regard the methods of Rainbow of Desire as extremely valuable in the sense that they offer tools to become aware of our own role in continuing vicious-circles of oppression. The oppressor is not *out there* anymore but lives inside of *me*, nourished by *my* own fears, which also implies that *I am* in power to transform it. I perceive these methods as an invitation to consciously move from being simply a victim of oppression towards honestly facing one's own inherent oppressor characteristics and consequently take self-responsibility. Apart from the original intention to understand psychological problems, the Rainbow of Desire techniques became useful tools to create characters in a play.[143]

Forum Theatre

Forum Theatre was developed in 1973 in Peru, as part of a literacy program.[144] Forum Theatre is certainly one of the most widely spread methods of Theatre of the Oppressed and is applied to various fields and issues. Its basic characteristic is to overcome the barrier between actresses and the audience within a theatrical action. Forum Theatre starts with the presentation of a scene which depicts a social problem that the audience can relate to. There is always at least one protagonist who faces oppression. The scene turns increasingly more conflictive and stops at the conflict's climax. This is the point when the spectators are invited to transform into *spect-actors* and *spect-actresses* by replacing the oppressed person and contributing their ideas of how to become free from that situation.

Forum-Theatre presents a scene or a play that must necessarily show a situation of oppression that the Protagonist does not know how to fight against, and fails. The spect-actors are invited to replace this Protagonist, and act out - on stage and not from the audience - all possible solutions, ideas, strategies. The other actors improvise the reactions of their characters facing each new intervention, so as to allow a sincere analysis of the real possibilities of using those sug-

---

142 Boal (1998): 149
143 Boal (2004)
144 Boal (2004)

gestions in real life. All spect-actors have the same right to intervene and play their ideas. Forum-Theatre is a collective rehearsal for reality.[145]

"What happens on stage, in the safety of the theatre, can become what he [Boal] calls a 'dress rehearsal' for trying to make actual change in real life."[146] This sentence highlights the potential which many Theatre of the Oppressed practitioners see in the Forum Theatre: The experience of once discovering a way out of an oppressive situation through an alternative strategy on stage, might encourage applying this strategy to reality as well.

Invisible Theatre

Invisible Theatre was picked up[147] by Boal in "Argentina, as political activity."[148] Invisible theatre is performed in public space and raises current and highly debated issues. It usually addresses hidden oppression or related topics which carry the potential to spark fierce discussions and aims at "making oppression visible".[149]

The actresses in this method do not declare themselves as actresses but play people who coincidentally pass by a sensational scene, which is also performed by actresses. The elaborated scene ought to trigger heavy reactions from the passers-by. Then one or some of the passing-by actors start to comment on the scene and discuss it loudly. They express their differing opinions and aim at producing a conflict between the people who have witnessed the scene. Some uninvolved witnesses might get involved and speak up. The idea behind this method is to raise critical topics and provoke thought about them. By these means of sparking a discussion, everyone could get an impulse to reflect on a certain topic, which might be uncomfortable to face. The confrontation with this topic possibly leaves the witnesses with inspiration, doubts, wonder or a slightly different perspective on that issue.

Invisible Theatre must not be disclosed after the hidden performance, in order to keep the situation realistic and not give the impression that the people have been made fun of. This subtle way of raising a discussion might reveal the most authentic opinions of people, other than if they were aware that they are part of a theatre. Embedding the formation of Invisible Theatre in its historical context, in

---

145 Boal (2004)
146 Bettencourt (2000)
147 Boal (1989): 116 Boal emphasized that it was not his invention but has always existed.
148 Boal (2004)
149 Boal (1989): 116 Translated by the author.

an era where critical and artistic expression of thoughts was violently suppressed, the need for an alternative channel to speak out critically, apart from the staged theatre appears logical. In this hidden way, critique was possible without the actors constantly running the danger to be imprisoned, kidnapped or tortured.

Invisible Theatre is a popular, yet highly debated method in the system of Theatre of the Oppressed. Barbara Frey explained different points of critique in her thesis from the year 1989.[150] If Invisible Theatre is not performed professionally and in a well prepared manner it carries the danger to reinforce prejudices. Frey also questions the tendency that an invisible theatre scene is often acted out only once instead of several times in different locations. Hence, she doubts that there are many sustainable and wide-ranging effects caused by this form of theatre. A further objection, which I agree with, is that performing Invisible Theatre implies responsibility. It carries the risk that in case people realize that the scene has been a theatrical farce, next time in a real situation, they might not see the necessity to take it serious or to take action either.

Legislative Theatre

Legislative Theatre was developed in the 1990s in Brazil, at the time when Augusto Boal had been elected to the *vereador*, member of the council in the sector of arts and culture, in Rio de Janeiro. In this position Boal could use "his political mandate to back changes to the law, or new laws, that they wished to see enacted."[151] Legislative Theatre is basically a forum theatre performance within which proposals for possible laws are elaborated. Consequently those suggestions are then formulated in juristic terms and brought into the parliamentarian process.[152] "During the period when Boal held office – from 1992 to 1996 – nineteen theatre groups were organised [and] thirteen laws were passed covering issues from sexual discrimination to the protection of crime witnesses."[153] The idea behind this method is to democratize politics and laws. "Legislative Theatre was born to help the Desire of the population to become Law – which it did at last 13 times."[154] These initiatives of encouraging the people to express their desires in order to implement them as laws faced strong resistance from different

150 Frey (1989): 62-69
151 Babbage (2004): 27
152 Dirnstorfer in Odierna (2006): 25
153 Babbage (2004): 29
154 Boal (2004)

sides, which included various verbal and violent attacks against the involved theatre groups.

Theatre of the Oppressed applied today

The methods of the system of Theatre of the Oppressed are generally regarded as flexible and easily accessible which is why it is practised nowadays in more than 70 countries.[155]

> There are Theatre of the Oppressed centres, groups and organisations in every continent – such as Jana Sanskriti (Calcutta), Headlines Theatre (Vancouver), Giolli (Italy), ATB (Burkina Faso), TOPLAB (New York), Formaat (Rotterdam) and Ashtar (Ramallah) – which use techniques directly or in combination with other strategies.[156]

Theatre of the Oppressed is applied in multi-facetted ways in diverse fields and issues, out of which the following examples are simply a fragmentary selection: Schools (Netherlands); Feminist/Women issues, domestic violence and health (India, Nepal); Conflict resolution (Israel, South Africa); Justice and penitentiary system, prisons (Brazil, Great Britain); development (Laos, Uganda, India), reconciliation (Bosnia-Herzegovina), integration, peace (Israel), homelessness (UK).[157] Theatre of the Oppressed methods have furthermore been applied to "political protest, education, therapy, [...] management and local government, as well as infiltrating the mainstream theatre establishment"[158]

Academic disciplines that deal with pedagogy, politics, psychology, science of theatre and Peace Studies[159] are those scientific fields in which an interest in Theatre of the Oppressed is most common.

155 Global Dialogue Series (2008)
156 Babbage (2004): 31
157 Theatre of the Oppressed (2008): "Evaluation & Reports" and "Yellow Pages"
158 Babbage (2004): 1
159 As for example in the MA Program for Peace Studies in Innsbruck (Austria) or at the University for Peace in Costa Rica.

Critical viewpoints on Theatre of the Oppressed

A lot has been written by and on Augusto Boal and the Theatre of the Oppressed. However, critique on Theatre of the Oppressed is rare, less elaborated and more difficult to find. For this reason, I approach the question of critique from mainly my own perspective on Theatre of the Oppressed, which is inspired by readings and personal practise.

Are unprejudiced, spontaneous and flexible dialogues possible?

Dialogue shall bring about change. There is no authority, no artist or politician who is in power to determine the outcome, but it is the dialogue between people that brings about a better solution. Boal often emphasises that the solution must not be predefined, not given by the actresses or directors to the spect-actors, but shall gradually evolve in a process of mutual dialogue. Thus, the first critical question that arises, which specifically refers to Forum Theatre, is about how free and flexible the dialogue can be and how predetermined the outcome actually is.

One aspect of limiting the scope of outcomes is the selection of spect-actors. Some forum theatre plays in Austria had an audience of a comparatively homogenous group, consisting mostly of friends of the actors or other Theatre of the Oppressed practitioners. In this case, the quest for alternative solutions occurs in quite a narrow frame of opinions. Additionally, it is often the case that a Forum play is performed only once, twice or very few times. In India, contrariwise, the group *Jana Sanskriti*[160] usually performs Forum Theatre plays dozens of times in different locations. This creates, on the one hand, a greater and more heterogeneous variety of people who get in touch with the forum, and on the other hand a greater spectrum of distinctive ideas that enrich the forum.

In any way I would say that a dialogue between actresses and spect-actresses is in fact often a dialogue between people who perceive themselves as belonging to the *oppressed*, rather than to the *oppressors*. I frequently felt a certain complicity

160 http://www.janasanskriti.org/

in these occasions, a kind of solidarity between the *oppressed*. However, there is hardly any dialogue with the so-called oppressors. Theatre of the Oppressed in general, and specifically Forum Theatre, aims at the empowerment of the oppressed. This is a clear positioning: It is very clear who is to be supported and it is clear who the oppressive counterpart that ought to be brought to realisation, is.

Theatre of the Oppressed is not about listening to all sides and dialoguing – it is not mediation. It rather dialogues to empower one side. Usually, the dialogue neither aims to reflect both sides, nor creates empathy for both positions, but mainly emphasises the strength of the oppressed. In my opinion, it makes sense that this intention is stated clearly, however, I struggle with a seemingly generous call for dialogue, which is in fact a horizontal dialogue between the oppressed. It seems to me that this form of dialogue is volitional and the vertical dialogue between oppressed and the oppressors is left out. This is a legitimate positioning of Theatre of the Oppressed, although I personally prefer the integration of all sides, *oppressed* and *oppressors*, into a process of questioning an oppressive situation.

I see a further fundamental, interesting contradiction within the practise of Theatre of the Oppressed. On the one hand there is a strong opposition against prejudices and generalisations, whether they are of racist, sexist, nationalist or other nature. On the other hand exists a clear judgemental distinction between oppressors/oppressed, good/bad, right/wrong. The contradiction here lies in the claim "we know that we know nothing" and everything has to be discovered together in dialogue, while at the same time there is the subtle, less obvious conviction that *we* do know, of course, who falls into which category: aware-unaware, oppressed-oppressor, just-unjust. There is in fact a strong, idealistic, in its origins Marxist thinking, which conflicts with the claim of being unprejudiced and hence totally open to learn from the *oppressed* – whatever issues, needs or proposals they bring up.

Possibly, this inherent contradiction in the practise of Theatre of the Oppressed is rooted in the biography of Augusto Boal. The first techniques were developed in South America, at a time when he was strongly influenced by socialist thought and his experiences during dictatorship. Back then, he only knew a total form of oppression, in which there was no doubt who is oppressed and who is an oppressor. In Europe Boal got in touch with a more subtle form of oppression: An oppression that was often internalized, less visible and more complex. There it became obvious that a person carries both facets in her, oppressor and oppressed.

Many of my arguments of critique and my difficulties to understand certain black-white aspects of Theatre of the Oppressed originate from the fact that I have personally never experienced an oppression of the first kind, as Boal did, but grew up in a reality where it is common sense that we all carry both facets in us.

> One ought to critically see that the scenes in Forum Theatre are far from reality. In order to stage reality, a situation is often reduced into a black-white schema: The portrayal of the counterparts oppressor – oppressed seems exaggerated. In fact, most situations in which oppression takes place, are so subtle, that only an accumulation of insignia of power point out the oppressor [...] – accordingly the counterpart is designed in a very powerless way.[161]

In this quote Barbara Frey criticizes the simplistic division between oppressors and oppressed and its exaggerated demonstration. Agreeing with her, I still believe that this critique is influenced by our personal experiences of a more subtle and complex kind of oppression as it is the case for most people in Europe.

Danger of manipulation?

The danger of manipulation becomes apparent especially in the method of *Invisible Theatre*. Arguments are prepared beforehand for both sides, protagonist and antagonist. However, of course the arguments which aim at supporting the protagonist shall "win" in the sense of convincing the unknowing audience. If passers-by involve and support the oppressed protagonist, the 'performance' is seen as success. Hence, it is very clear what the favoured outcome would be. This is fine. I believe that in order to reach a goal, the goal has to be clarified from the beginning. However, it is not exactly a spontaneous dialogue if the actresses have prepared their arguments and the passers-by have not. From my point of view, it is more honest to state at the beginning, within the group, that there is one preferred outcome, instead of declaring meekly that this 'under-cover performance' is only for the sake of *exploring* different established opinions within society.

---

161 Frey (1989): 60 Translated by the author. „Kritisch muss man auch die Realitätsfremdheit der Modellszenen beim Forumtheater betrachten: Um die Wirklichkeit darzustellen, wird eine Situation oft in ein Schwarz-weiß Schema gepresst: Die Zeichnung der Kontrahenten Unterdrücker – Unterdrückter wirkt übertrieben.Tatsächlich sind die meisten Situationen, in denen Unterdrückung stattfindet, so subtil, dass erst eine Anhäufung der Machtinsignien auf eine Unterdrückerfigur die Unterdrückungssituation verdeutlichet- dementsprechend machtlos wird die Gegenfigur gestaltet."

In *Forum Theatre*, it is in the hands of the *joker*, who is the mediator between the audience and the actresses, to influence the outcome through the questions he poses. This is in my opinion no drawback, yet it ought to be remembered that the result has been influenced by the joker's selective questioning.

Who shall be transformed?

I think that the attitude of the group which prepares a forum-play makes the most profound difference. Some might enter the process with the willingness that they themselves become transformed, learn and raise their own awareness, and then get into dialogue with others to learn even more. Others might use Forum Theatre mainly as a tool for activism and aim at raising awareness within those who are *unaware*.

There is a thin line between the first approach, which is primarily a personal quest for consciousness followed by the will to get in dialogue and the second approach that carries strong paternalistic and missionary characteristics. If the major goal is to liberate others and open the eyes of the unknowing, this carries an intrinsic arrogance towards those who are reputed as *unaware*. Here one easily falls back into the trap of becoming an oppressor herself.

I observed that many times both attitudes exist in an individual or in a group of Theatre of the Oppressed practitioners. This antagonism is interesting, as possibly every person has experiences of knowledge in one moment, while in the next moment becomes aware of one's own ignorance. Even though this contradiction exists in many of us, I mention it here because it is too easy to become caught up again in the vicious circle of oppression, which starts with believing *to know the truth* while proudly thinking of oneself as one of the good guys.

A person carries out *acts* of oppression, but *is* not an Oppressor

Can we speak of a *person* who *is* an oppressor or an oppressed? Certainly nobody falls into either category by nature, but rather one carries out acts of oppression in one situation while being oppressed in another. Hence, it is the *situation* in which one is *acting* oppressively or is oppressed. Even those who rank the highest in terms of (political, financial, physical) power might turn into oppressed in their relationships or by internal fears. Therefore I think we all carry the potential of both sides in us and there is no human being which can be reduced to just one category.

It is more complex, maybe too complex to stage an oppressive situation in all its facets. In theatre reduction is inevitable! However, it is possible to scrutinize the language within Theatre of the Oppressed. It does make a difference whether we call a person an oppressor or whether we state clearly that he or she oppresses in a given situation or by performing a certain action. Hence, the actions of people would be criticized, not the people as such. I would favour this shift in talking about oppression, because it could break open the judgemental, categorizing duality between good/bad or oppressive/oppressed *people*.

Use of the term 'oppression' as welcome provocation?

The term is a provocation. If so much discussion is going on about it, why not accept it as a name that is difficult to ignore, a name that rarely triggers indifference? This is one point of view. Another point of view is my assumption that concentrating on oppression possibly reinforces the vicious circle of oppression by emphasising it endlessly. If I focus my attention on oppression, might it be strengthened? I am convinced that it makes a difference whether I continuously hypnotise myself by declaring that I am ill compared to confirming to myself that I am healthy – even though the illness might be a *fact* just as oppression. In this argumentation it would also make a difference whether one perpetually affirms her identity of an *oppressed* rather than of a *free* person. David Diamond for example calls his form of theatre "Theatre for Living"[162], which clearly has a more positive, life-affirming notion than Theatre of the Oppressed.

I would now suggest changing the label "Theatre of the Oppressed" into a more positive term, into one which expresses more of a desired outcome, such as 'Theatre of the Free'. But, I understand that a title which mentions oppression is already a critical, political statement and serves to attract people who are interested in criticising certain social structures.

Use of Theatre of the Oppressed tools

Theatre of the Oppressed is a compilation of methods with ethic principles at its base. It is a tool which has been applied to various contexts and thereby often used with a fundamentally different attitude than originally intended. For example, if companies organize Forum Theatre plays in order to collect ideas on how to reduce costs, increase sales or to find out which employee works most efficiently or who would better be dismissed, it is not Theatre of the Oppressed anymore.

162 Diamond (2007)

Even though the tools appear similar, the attitude is fundamentally different. If such reasons motivate the application of Theatre of the Oppressed, this is an abuse of its methods and is no longer in accordance with Theatre of the Oppressed.

This problem of deciding how to apply Theatre of the Oppressed in a *correct* way proves once more that often a tool itself is innocent, but rather it is the attitude by which it is used that determines its consequences. Therefore, I propose that instead of spending much time on criticizing certain ways of applying these basically neutral methods, one should better make use of Theatre of the Oppressed as a fundament upon which to construct one's own special form. David Diamond in Canada, Hector Aristízabal in the United States, and Sanjoy Ganguly in India are just a few examples for individuals who created their own outstanding fusions of Theatre of the Oppressed, combined with other methods of their personal interests.

Conclusion

It is the same form of division between the oppressors and the oppressed as it is between those who have the power to judge and those who are judged; those who elect and those who are elected; those who create and those who consume; those who educate and those who get educated or those who act and those who watch. Boal turns against all of these divisions which peg some people as active and others as passive. Instead, Boal calls for becoming *spect-actors*, which means that instead of apathetically accepting certain structures the way they are – even though suffering from them – to get actively involved and interact with one's environment in a creative way. And he calls for learning with and from one another, in a mutual dialogue, in order not to allow placing the responsibility for one's life or knowledge onto any so-called authority that claims to know the *truth*. In this aspect Augusto Boal's attitude, which has been largely influenced by Paulo Freire, comes close to Osho's and Krishnamurti's understanding of learning. Learning means not to blindly believe any authority, but rather to find out one's own truth.

Theatre of the Oppressed calls for positioning oneself, to take a stand even though the momentary opinion might shift. Taking a clear position and having the courage to speak out one's mind is crucial for dialogue. As Theatre of the Oppressed has the courage to do so, it is possible to also spot certain inherent contradictions and conflicts and to shed a critical light on it. Concluding, I think that it is the core of Theatre of the Oppressed to refrain from believing to own the *philosopher's stone*, as Boal mentioned in the foreword of the German version of "Theatre of the Oppressed". Hence, I suggest that all who work with it ought to be aware of the omnipresent danger of falling back into the trap of arrogance, the thought that the eyes of the *others* have to be opened, while oneself is all knowing!

In the next step the topics 'Theatre of the Oppressed' and 'Freedom' will be connected.

THEATRE OF THE OPPRESSED AND FREEDOM

Introduction

As Freedom is the first pillar in my thesis and Theatre of the Oppressed is the second I regard it necessary to construct an associative bridge between the two. I will shortly overview communalities as well as contradictions between my definition of freedom – inspired by Krishnamurti and Osho – and the understanding of freedom within the Theatre of the Oppressed. First, I will describe how freedom is understood from the perspective of Augusto Boal and Paulo Freire. Subsequently I examine what their understanding of freedom has in common with the ideas of Krishnamurti and Osho and where contradictions can be detected. Secondly, I analyse "The Rainbow of Desire" and search for aspects within this Theatre of the Oppressed method, which directly aims at a discovery of more inner freedom.

FREEDOM FROM A THEATRE OF THE OPPRESSED PERSPECTIVE

Freedom and Discipline

> Theatre of the Oppressed is the *Game of Dialogue*: we play and learn together. All kinds of Games must have *Discipline* - clear rules that we must follow. At the same time, Games have absolute need of creativity and *Freedom*. TO is the perfect synthesis between the antithetic *Discipline* and *Freedom*. Without Discipline, there is no Social Life; without Freedom, there is no Life.
>
> The *Discipline* of our Game is our belief that we that we must re-establish the right of everyone to exist in dignity. We believe that all of us are more, and much better, than what we think we are. We believe in solidarity.
>
> Our *Freedom* is to invent ways to help to humanize Humanity, freely invading all fields of human activities: social, pedagogical, political, artistic... Theatre is a Language and so it can be used to speak about all human concerns, not to be limited to theatre itself.[163]

---

163 Boal (2004)

This is an interesting aspect of freedom raised by Augusto Boal. Similar to Osho's argument that freedom goes hand in hand with responsibility, Boal claims that freedom and discipline are antithetic and hence both are equally essential. What would freedom be good for if it lacks the orientation of discipline? "Without Discipline, there is no Social Life; without Freedom, there is no Life", Boal claims. In this statement seeming opposites turn out to actually need and enrich each other. The dance of discipline and freedom is a balancing act between compromising for the common good on the one hand – as it is obviously not constructive to behave like a crowd of egoistic individuals – and keeping one's individual freedom alive, daring to move beyond certain norms that define how the 'common good' has to be, on the other hand.

Freedom and Idealism?

"Our *Freedom* is to invent ways to help to humanize Humanity." This and innumerable other statements by Boal or Freire express their idealist thinking. Both believe that the creative potential is hidden in all of us and simply needs to be dug out. At the same they tend to create ideals of solidarity, humanity, non-violence and others which show that they do hope for a better world in the future. Both promote a change towards a more peaceful community of humans. For Krishnamurti, and I claim that Osho would agree, ideals are projections, which

> serve the people to get distracted from their own problems and conflicts. [...] The people cover up their character features with the opposite of what they are: They are violent, so they invent the ideal of non-violence. They hate, so they make love become an ideal. They are internally insecure and confused, so they strive for security and order.[164]

Even though the words of Freire and Boal appear similar to those of Osho and Krishnamurti, I observed that, especially in their earlier writings, they were passionately and non-violently fighting for better circumstances in the future – and they seemed to desperately want to escape the situation in the *here and now*. This might be understandable regarding the context of their writings, which was during a military dictatorship in Brazil that was executing daily violence.

164 Dietrich (2008): 334 Translated by the author.

Another element of their idealism is the oppression of certain character features. While reading Boal's and Freire's first books, I wondered: Where do you speak about the violence inside of us; the oppressive features of each one of us; the aggression well hidden behind our masks of solidarity; the violent, pejorative, angry or arrogant thoughts that we are all capable of? Suppressing these facets of our characters by creating ideals of *peacefulness* is the perfect engine to propel a vicious circle of judging others without honestly looking at oneself. Or, in the words of Osho:

> We suppress the love for our enemies, and we suppress the hatred against our friends. We suppress! [...] Transformation can not emerge from oppression. [...] The so-called 'non-violent people' are the ugliest people in the world. They are no good people, because they sit on a volcano.[165]

Inspired by Khalil Gibran's question "For how can a tyrant rule the free and the proud, but for a tyranny in their own freedom and a shame in their own pride?"[166], I think that not a single oppressive political systems would exist, if there was not a society that was absorbed in oppressive thoughts. Governments simply reflect the tendencies of a society. (In "The Rainbow of Desire" Boal increasingly looked at the problems of oppressing feelings and thoughts inside of us.)

Altogether, I see a fundamental contradiction in their understandings of freedom which conflicts around the issue of idealism. For Osho "[t]he origin of tension is the *becoming*. The human being always tries to become different as it is [...] Tension comes from the hypothetical, not yet realized possibilities."[167] Hence, freedom is a relaxed way of being in the moment. For Paulo Freire and Augusto Boal, however, the idea of *becoming* and the hope in the change for the better are the driving forces behind their life-works.

165 Osho in Dietrich (2008): 343 Translated by the author.
166 Gibran (2008)
167 Osho in Dietrich (2008): 342 Translated and italicised by the author.

Freedom from oppressive images and freedom as condition

> The oppressed, having internalized the image of the oppressor and adopted its guidelines, are fearful of freedom. Freedom would require them to eject this image and replace it with autonomy and responsibility. Freedom is acquired by conquest, not by gift. It must be pursued constantly and responsibly. Freedom is not an ideal located outside of man; nor is it an idea which becomes a myth. It is rather the indispensable condition for the quest of human completion.[168]

This quote of Paulo Freire carries two essential messages which both show similarities with my definition of freedom. The first is the idea of freeing oneself from oppressive images that we keep in our heads, which curtail us and prevent us from living the lives we want and taking full responsibility for the choices we make. In this quote, as well as in the methods of "The Rainbow of Desire", Freire and Boal address the issue of internalized oppression which is less visible from the outside, yet possibly more substantial.

The second message is that freedom is not an ideal, but rather an indispensable condition for human completion. (I am personally very sceptical whether something like "human completion" exists, or if it is yet another ideal to strive for.) However, I find it interesting that Osho, who distinguished between *freedom from* and *freedom for*, also perceived freedom merely as the fertile ground on which something else might grow and blossom. Both see freedom as the precondition – we might call it *free-condition* – for constructing something greater, whether it is human completion for Freire or creativity for Osho. Freedom in this sense is neither a goal nor anything of substance, but a starting point. Freedom is the white canvas which invites us to become artists and upon which we can paint our lives.

Freedom and authenticity

"The oppressed suffer from the duality which has established itself in their innermost being. They discover that without freedom they cannot exist authentically. Yet, although they desire authentic existence, they fear it."[169] Freedom is to

---

168 Freire (1996): 29
169 Freire (1996): 30

have the courage and the self-confidence to live authentically. Osho described freedom as the *courage to be yourself.*

Freedom is to trust one's own cognition

"Liberation is a praxis: the action and reflection of men and women upon their world in order to transform it. [...] Liberating education consists in acts of cognition, not transferrals of information."[170] Paulo Freire and Augusto Boal repeatedly highlighted that liberation comes from authentic realisations and processes of cognition within oneself and not through studying and storing certain information. This conviction goes together with Krishnamurti's and Osho's calls for finding out our own truth instead of believing or following authorities.

All four of them share an attitude which emphasises the creative potential of every individual, its capacity to live authentically and to critically scrutinize ideas which are generally promoted as truth. Similarly, in the words of Erich Fromm "the freedom to create and to construct, to wonder and to venture [...] requires the individual be active and responsible, not a slave or a well-fed cog in the machine."[171]

"The Rainbow of Desire" and inner freedom

Resignation

> Most of the images of the oppressed made by the oppressed themselves are images of resignation. They are not images of defeat in a battle. [...] Lack of action, going round in circles, the inability to break through an aggressive situation, these are, in general, consequences of the absence of an ideal image. It is much easier to leave if we know where we want to go to. [172]

In a workshop in Croatia in 2008, Boal mentioned that he likes to make theatre with the oppressed, whereas it is extremely difficult to work with people who are stuck in a victim-identity and who have already given up. Resignation does not

170 Freire (1996): 60
171 Fromm in Freire (1996): 50
172 Boal (1998): 86f

allow constructive action. Therefore many of the Theatre of the Oppressed methods use the creation of ideal images to spark the driving energy indispensable for changing oppressive circumstances. In this aspect, Theatre of the Oppressed enhances the discovery of inner freedom, as getting out of a passive state of resignation and self-pity is the first step to become free in a broader sense.

Masks

> If it is true that the rituals of daily life force each of us to don the appropriate, adequate mask, that is to say, a mask whose function is to cushion the collisions between people and the actions they are called on to carry out, or obliged to carry out, then equally it must be true the ritual, or considerably modify it, or even reveal its inadequacy. In fact, a struggle rages between the ritual and the person, and the mask is the result of this struggle.[173]

As authenticity is an essential facet of feeling free, certain Rainbow of Desire games and techniques are valuable as they raise awareness about masks that we unconsciously don to hide our true feelings, thoughts, fears, anger or other less welcome features.

Fear

> A man without fear can be eliminated, assassinated, but never oppressed. [...] For fear of losing our jobs, we submit to unacceptable conditions of work. For fear of losing a person's love or company we accept unacceptable situations. Out of fear of death, we accept ways of life we don't like. We are afraid, always [...] We are conscious of fear, to a greater or lesser extent, or not at all. But fear is always present, on the lookout, conditioning our actions and reactions, conditioning our lives.[174]

This quote of Augusto Boal could have easily been said by Krishnamurti or Osho as well. It is fear which hypnotises us to believe that we have to accept situations which are not satisfying. It is, for example, the fear of loneliness or failure that seductively whispers into our ears something like "don't risk losing that ... it could always become worse!" The consequence is that people feel unfree and convince themselves to be victims, hopelessly trapped in their circumstances.

---

173 Boal (1998): 133
174 Boal (1998): 118

This is the opposite of freedom: The lack of courage or hope to actively transform frustrating conditions; shirking responsibility for one's own life; and reducing one's freedom of creatively shaping one's life to an existence of moaning complaint and self-pitying grievance.

"The Rainbow of Desire" of all Theatre of the Oppressed methods, especially enhances self-reflection and thereby works with the responsibility that we have for ourselves. One example is the technique of 'cops in the head', which tries to illuminate images in our heads which (as mentioned before in chapter III.5.1.3) oblige "us to do what we don't want to do or prevent[s] us from doing what we do want to do."[175] Such a *cop*, such an internalized instance, could be the image of mother, father, relatives or friends saying "you *should* not...!", "you *have to* be...!", "you will never be able to...!" It could be an image of a representative of cultural, religious, moral norms or values which reaffirms sore conscience within you. Or, it could as well be the voice of fear which functions as a *cop in the head.* Consequently, working with such internalized instances which allow and re-establish external oppression facilitates a discovery of more freedom.

Conclusion

The understanding of freedom from Boal's and Freire's perspective has certain communalities with Osho's and Krishnamurti's concept of freedom. What Osho and Krishnamurti call responsibility, Boal defines as discipline. From my point of view, they all say that the one side of the coin is freedom, whereas the other is reliability and the responsibility of using one's freedom creatively. All four agree that trusting one's own cognition instead of looking up to so-called authorities is an integral part of freedom. Furthermore, they all speak about internalized oppression and internalized concepts as a hindrance to freedom.

The main aspect in which I perceive disagreement is the following: Osho's and Krishnamurti's emphasis on getting free from ideals and projections into the future contradicts clearly with Boal's and Freire's idealism of a more peaceful, solidary, less oppressive and more human humanity.

In the next step I will look at Theatre of the Oppressed as it is applied in prisons. Augusto Boal, who had been to prison himself before being forced into exile, claims:

---

175 Boal (1998): 149

> Metaphorically, the Theatre of the Oppressed was born in prison. I like to say: in this kind of theatre, the citizen – in the present – studies the past and invents the future. The stage, the arena, like the cell or the prison yard can be a place of study; and the theatre can be a fit instrument, a proper language for that discourse, that quest for oneself.[176]

Augusto Boals's time in prison was a time of deep (self-)reflection, learning and politicisation. Yet, this is rather an exception than the norm. I deem it useful and necessary to practise Theatre of the Oppressed in prisons, hence, I will delve deeper into that topic in the consequent chapter.

176 Boal (2001): 298

THEATRE OF THE OPPRESSED IN PRISON

Introduction

For almost twenty years the methods of Theatre of the Oppressed have been applied to prisons in various countries around the world. In 2001 the project *Staging Human Rights* carried out workshops and staged Forum and Legislative Theatre scenes on human rights issues in 34 prisons in the State of São Paulo, Brazil.[177] More than 2000 participants attended the various activities and more than 2000 spect-actors were present during performances. The methods applied in that large-scale project are currently implemented in over 100 prisons in Brazil. This project was run in partnership with FUNAP, the organisation which manages the São Paolo prison's education system, the People's Palace Projects in London and the CTO Rio[178], the Centre of Theatre of the Oppressed in Rio de Janeiro.

Almost ten years before, in 1992, James Thompson and Paul Heritage set up the TiPP Centre, Theatre in Prisons and Probation Centre, in the UK. In cooperation with the University of Manchester's Drama Department, the TiPP Centre organized and carried out theatre workshops in prisons and probation, undertook research and published "books and articles about art initiatives in the criminal justice system."[179] Over the years they specialised on practical theatre work and left the research to the Centre for Applied Theatre Research.

Staging Human Rights has possibly been the largest-scale project in which the methods of Theatre of the Oppressed have ever been applied to prisons. The TiPP centre is a very important, long-run organisation in terms of arranging the implementation of theatre into the penitentiary system. Most of the literature which I found and used for my research had been published by authors from the TiPP centre or by interrelated people and projects. A further important source of my information has been the Theatre of the Oppressed homepage and its reports, as well as personal contact with individuals who facilitate workshops in prisons.

---

177 Theatre of the Oppressed (2009): Prison Theatre
178 Centro de Teatro do Oprimido: See http://www.ctorio.org.br/
179 TiPP: TiPP History

In Germany, Italy, Croatia, the United States of America, the Netherlands, Israel and Austria, Theatre of the Oppressed has – at least temporarily – entered prisons. It is a common practise to combine Theatre of the Oppressed methods with other theatre techniques such as improvisational theatre and working with masks, psychological methods such as psychodrama, cognitive behavioural theory[180] or drama therapy. For this reason it is difficult to draw a strict line between Theatre of the Oppressed prison projects and others. Rarely a prison theatre project declares itself explicitly as a Theatre of the Oppressed project. There are many prison theatres around the world which have nothing in common with Theatre of the Oppressed. There are, at the same time, prison theatre workshops which use only a few of the warming-up games of Boal's book "Games for Actors and Non-Actors"[181]. And there are prison theatre programs which make use of Augusto Boal's simple games as well as bigger methods from the Theatre of the Oppressed arsenal such as Image theatre, Forum theatre, the Rainbow of Desire, Cops in the Head or Newspaper theatre. In my research I focus on those projects who openly declare a connection with such bigger methods and with the principles of Theatre of the Oppressed.

Objectives

What are the common objectives for the application of Theatre of the Oppressed to prisons? What are the motivations of practitioners to engage with a social setting, away from common, professional theatre companies? Is it that "artists and creatives who rage against the system, turn instinctively to others who rage. For there is a reluctance in us to channel personal creativity into products that simply oil the sophisticated clockwork of consumerism", as Chris Johnston admits?[182]

Obviously many artists and theatre makers feel attracted to make pioneer work, in the sense to work with men and women who have never been trained as

180 See Blagg (2003): Principally Maguire & Priestley "Offending Behaviour: Skills and strategems for going Straight" (1985)

181 Boal (1992)

182 Johnston in Balfour (2004): 107

actors or actresses and who nevertheless, or maybe just because of that, might experience a groundbreaking discovery of their own creative potential. It is their stories, their conflicts, and their issues which make the topic for theatre play. Prison theatre, as well as other forms of *applied theatre*[183], combine artistic, aesthetic processes with social issues. As I observed, the sharp edge on which to balance these two poles – creative expression for the sake of art and social action – carries its great, fascinating potential as well as its greatest vulnerability towards criticism. In the following I will explore common objectives for the implementation of Theatre of the Oppressed to prisons.

Giving prisoners a voice to express their feelings and their stories

Prisoners are partly seen as oppressed by a system which decided that putting them behind bars would be the best solution for society. Theatre of the Oppressed with prison inmates moves away from questions of guilt, judgement, punishment or mercy towards inspiring self-reflection and self-expression. "[T]heatre offers the possibility that prisoners who are the objects of the system's vigilance and society's denunciations can begin to look and to speak as subjects in their own lives."[184] In most Theatre of the Oppressed prison projects the final forum play has been developed by a long process of discussing personal experiences of the participants, then projecting these onto a fictitious protagonist character (thereby it becomes easier to talk indirectly about oneself) and then finally acting it out. Eventually the play is the result of everyone's story and ideas combined. In the safe space of theatre participants often dare to express their genuine feelings and thoughts more openly.

Discovering the inner, hidden creative potential through theatre

Paolo Freire said about the oppressed: "So often do they hear that they are good for nothing, know nothing and are incapable of learning anything – that they are sick, lazy, and unproductive – that in the end they become convinced of their own unfitness."[185] Instead of shattering the self-esteem of people in prison even more by emphasising their issues, mistakes or *failures*, Theatre of the Oppressed

183 See Balfour (2009)
184 Heritage in Balfour (2004): 195
185 Freire (1996): 45

challenges the participant's creative thinking and invites them to make careful steps beyond their limits. One important motive of Theatre of the Oppressed is its aim at supporting the realisation that everyone is capable of being creative, of having spontaneous great ideas and can act them out. Participants experience themselves from a side which they possibly never discovered before. Often acting and performing in front of others are special challenges because the one who acts becomes visible and suddenly gains an unfamiliar lot of attention. Furthermore, an experience of recognizing one's own courage in a challenging situation can strengthen the trust in oneself.

Raising consciousness about personal coping strategies

Theatre of the Oppressed in prison does not primarily aim at a momentary better mood, but at triggering a process of becoming conscious of one's own coping strategies with fear, anger, sadness, aggression, loneliness or other feelings and experimenting with alternative ways to deal with them, without causing harm to oneself or others. Forum theatre provides a forum to explore and practise alternative behaviour strategies that might have more satisfying and healthy consequences. 'Cop in the Head' and the 'Rainbow of Desire' are techniques which are useful for looking at internalized hindrances or at one's scope of desires and needs. Within all these methods "it's the discussion about alternatives that is empowering, because it gives every single participant the freedom to make her own choices instead of following a stereotyped reaction pattern."[186]

Raising consciousness about social and economical contradictions

Crime is more than merely a mistaken, pathological act of an individual – crime is logically embedded in its social and economical context. "We want that also those ones who live in prison get involved actively"[187], Bárbara Santos from CTO Rio explains. One motivation of Theatre of the Oppressed practitioners to work in prisons might therefore be to further *conscientização*[188]. This means to identify together with the prisoners social and economic contradictions, and con-

186 Matthijssen (2007): 28
187 Santos in Baumann (2003): 1 Translated by the author.
188 See chapter III.3.2.

sequently speaking out against such discriminating circumstances or making them public by the means of theatre performances.

Apart from the effects on the inmates and workshop facilitators directly, it is also about sparking a public debate about prisons. For this reason prison forum theatre plays often invite people from the outside or, as practised in Brazil, prison theatre groups often tour and perform in public spaces, at universities or at cultural centres. In Brazil, activities are carried out initially "with the prisoners only, then with prisoners and prison staff together and then with people from the outside who come to the performances. Eventually the inmates go to the public."[189] In this way more people get involved in discussions about oppressive conditions in prisons and in society in general. Consequently some might become more conscious and act upon these insights.

Improving the relationships inside the prisons

Another objective that is desired is to improve the relationships inside the prison, among prisoners on the one hand, and between prisoners and guards on the other hand. A system of oppression and violence between or against prisoners only strengthens the mistrust and aggression in the whole institution. If there was, on the contrary, an atmosphere of more mutual trust and respect between all counterparts it would certainly improve the conditions of prison-life. Therefore, one objective for practitioners of the *TheaterDialog* group in Germany has been "encouraging self-reflection and the strengthening of teamwork capacities"[190]. In which ways the relationships in prison have changed after doing theatre work together will be explained in the chapter about effects. Before, however, I will depict frequently occurring challenges when applying Theatre of the Oppressed to prisons.

---

189 Santos in Baumann (2003): 1 Translated by the author.
190 Wolf and Baumann (2004): 7 Translated by the author.

CHALLENGES

The challenges that Theatre of the Oppressed practitioners face when working in prison are manifold while at the same time it seems that all of them struggle with the same specific issues. I observed three categories of challenges: The challenges with the prison institution, challenges during the workshops and the challenge of appropriate evaluation.

Challenges with the prison institution

> [I]n any system designed by some to control others, there will almost always be a space for resistance, a fissure in which to forge at least a little freedom. [...] That is why creative work which produces and exploits them is customarily an unwelcome challenge to authority, an unpredictable disruption of norms, a kind of playing with fire.[191]

Obviously, the first challenge is to enter the institution. "Of course we had to 'package' the program a little to get it past the guardians – we could not quite say out loud that we wanted to work with prisoners on practising ways they could resist oppression."[192] When there are two mindsets clashing – a justice system constructed to punish and keep society in control (or let us ironically say: in *security*), with artists who generally tend to question boundaries, create ways to cross them and themselves do not want to be controlled by so-called authorities – it is of little surprise that misunderstandings and mutual prejudices complicate cooperation.

"Drama tends to have a bad reputation in prisons. It is seen as something that stirs the prisoners up. Drama workers are seen as difficult and demanding, with no understanding of why security is important"[193], as Sally Stamp describes the prejudices she frequently faced. On the other hand theatre practitioners often

191 Kershaw in Balfour (2004): 35
192 Bettencourt (2000): 1f
193 Stamp in Thompson (1998): 107

criticize the penitentiary system and hence meet prison staff in a prejudiced way as well. Practitioners often perceive prison staff as accomplices of an oppressive institution on whose goodwill they nevertheless depend. This dichotomy shows the common conflict of prison theatre makers who resist the criminal justice system while at the same time seek fissures to exist in it.

Often the work in prisons for Theatre of the Oppressed practitioners is complicated by guards who have the job to be present during the theatre work. Sometimes they interfere with critical comments or they are simply present, watching the process with a sceptical facial expression. For many guard's points of view, drama is seen as a waste of time and an unnecessary security risk. However, there are Theatre of the Oppressed projects – such as *Staging Human Rights* in Brazil – which consciously aims at integrating prison guards into the theatre process, or who do extra theatre trainings with them. This I find a good, tangible way of demonstrating the benefits of theatre work.

The rigid rule to ask for permission for any special equipment needed in the workshop, sometimes days in advance, impedes carrying out spontaneous ideas. The fluctuation of participants, who are either released, relocated to other prisons, not allowed to continue the theatre work for other reasons, or coming too late to practise due to special checkups by the prison staff, is a further common challenge that endangers the stability and continuity of any participating group.

Above all, the lack of money and financial support is possibly the most prevalent challenge. Ivana Marijancic from Croatia states that they received "no money support from the government to continue with workshops, even if they saw benefice from that"[194]. Jenny Hughes who facilitated theatre projects in women's prisons in the UK explains that the "fundamental dilemma facing the practitioner is an economic one and relates to how he or she can make a living doing this sort of work."[195]

Challenges within the workshop

There are other challenges which occur within the theatre process, in the group, or between group and workshop leaders. A common difficulty is the lack of trust.

---

194 Marijancic in Under Pressure (2008): 20
195 Hughes in Thompson (1998): 61

> Prisoners have many reasons to be distrustful. Some will have been informed on by co-defendants, friends or family. Often they will have had difficult family experiences and many will have been in care. Part of the work will be in developing the capacity to trust. As this happens people feel vulnerable and consequently may distance themselves, not attend, or leave the group.[196]

Openness might be used against oneself. Showing emotions is feared as it could lead to being laughed at, ridiculed, bullied or called a wimp. For this reason many theatre exercises and games played in the beginning, aim at building trust. Usually mistrust vanishes over a period of working together in a group. Sometimes there is mistrust against workshop leaders, because it might not be the first time that artists came to the prison and did their *experiments* with the inmates and then left them again "feeling manipulated or exploited".[197]

Furthermore, a common issue is that the personal problems of the participants which come up during the theatre work might be too difficult to deal with. Sometimes memories of traumatic situations arise and the theatre practitioners are not psychologically or therapeutically trained – or lack of time and workshop personnel does not allow focussing on the struggles of one individual person. This challenge is often tackled by good collaboration between theatre practitioners and the prison psychologists or social workers. "Within the prisons the practise of dialogue is not valued neither stimulated. [...] Communication is reduced to the confrontation of monologues that neither interpenetrate nor influence each other."[198] Therefore, the shift towards genuine dialogue is a further challenge, yet it is the base for all cooperation within a theatrical process.

Challenge of evaluation

One challenge here might be, as mentioned in an evaluation of a drama based offending behaviour workshop in England, that "[…] people [are sometimes] saying what they think you want to hear. [...] young people are aware that the outcome of their order may be decided on them giving appropriate or acceptable rather than congruent or detailed responses."[199] "Prisoners may think that if they get involved they will get benefits, they think it will affect their home leave",

196 Stamp in Thompson (1998): 106
197 Mazzini, Robert: Interview with the author in December 2008.
198 Santos in Under Pressure (2008): 4
199 BLAGG (2003): 4

Sally Stamp[200] points out. The possibility that the seemingly safe space of theatre is nevertheless influenced by the inmate's fear of being too honest and thus will suffer the consequences from it, ought to be taken into account when evaluations are conducted.

"If we want to make valid statements about the success of the program, the participants should be monitored for at least their remaining sentence plus a year after release."[201] Would participants agree with that expanded time-span of monitoring? Who would finance that?

EFFECTS

After dealing with the objectives and the challenges of applying Theatre of the Oppressed to prisons I will now point out certain effects which I frequently encountered in my research. These effects, however, are mostly described by theatre workshop facilitators themselves and not by the participants. From time to time I came across single quotes from participants, yet of all the literature on Theatre of the Oppressed in prisons I have not found a single article written by a prisoner. Thompson's anthology on 'Prison Theatre', includes two articles by inmates who described their experiences with theatre in prison, yet the majority of reports lack the voice's of the participants themselves, which from my point of view is one of the most crucial elements in Boal's and Freire's original ideas. So, as my research is based on literature, I have to admit that almost all reported effects which I am going to mention now were documented by facilitators and not by the people themselves! Therefore, I ask you to keep this specific perspective in mind when reading about the supposed effects.

200 Stamp in Thompson (1998): 107
201 Mattijssen (2007): 13

Relationships within the prison change

> Out of everything that makes up this unit, the thing that costs nothing in terms of money is staff and prisoners getting together and talking; it is the one thing that has brought about results. The emphasis is placed on seeing the individual as a person in his own right without relying on labelling or categorisation in order to identify.[202]

This quote originates from a prisoner in South Africa, after a conflict transformation course. Although the quote did not originally refer to a Theatre of the Oppressed workshop, these words express the essence of manifold other statements on how the relationships within the prison transform through theatre. Very often theatre projects bring staff and prisoners together in a dialogue for the first time and Theatre of the Oppressed aim is at letting go of labelling and categorisations to be able to truly see the person behind.

Luc Opdebeeck from the Dutch group *Formaat* observed that there was "enormous mutual support of women who barely knew each other."[203] Within the workshop and after, changes in the physical contact between the inmates have been noticed by Katrin Wolf and Till Baumann during their work with youth offenders at the Justizanstalt Raßnitz in Germany.[204] Physical closeness increased and was interpreted as a sign of mutual trust.

"As one prisoner reaches across to touch another, you know that a contact is being made that only happens because of this activity we call theatre, and it is in direct contradiction to the ways in which people are meant to relate within that space."[205] In this quote Paul Heritage acknowledges that one powerful effect of prison theatre is that suddenly there is a contact. A connection between one another is built up that has not existed before.

Self-reflection and discovery of alternative behaviour strategies

"[I]n the subsequent discussion with the young inmates it became clear, that with the method of a theatre-pedagogical approach critical examination of one's own

---

202 Balfour (2004): 15
203 Opdebeeck in Under Pressure (2008): 18
204 Wolf and Baumann (2004^2): 15 Translated by the author.
205 Heritage in Balfour (2004): 200

life-situation and criminal development was made possible"[206]. This quote by the director of the prison for young offenders in Raßnitz, Germany, expresses that self-reflection has been facilitated and increased through the theatre process. Becoming clearer of one's own boundaries and developing the courage to transgress them, was an integral part of the workshop process, as Wolf and Baumann explained.[207]

Expressing oneself

One effect that has been documented frequently is that the courage and ability to articulate oneself increased throughout the theatre process. The social worker Larisch commented after a project conducted by Wolf and Baumann and that the male adolescents "practised mutual regard and consideration and some got the opportunity to express himself without being hindered by personal or intellectual shortcomings."[208] "The theatre offered a different kind of emotionally revelatory language, a way of developing relationships not based on power and control"[209], which Alon and Kufitnec noticed at the end of the nine month program with male prisoners and female students. Jenny Hughes documented some of the feedback of women prisoners who participated in a Blagg! workshop.

> I learnt to talk about myself in front of others without getting embarrassed...', 'I am less confused than I was...', [...] 'you know you're taking part and you have to use your brains before speaking...', 'it makes me understand my life, I had to do this to see how I was living...[210]

All those statements show that Theatre of the Oppressed methods facilitate the individual's capability for expressing thoughts, feelings, issues and visions. These quotes also point out that a profound process of self-reflection occurred through theatre work. The methods of Theatre of the Oppressed and especially Forum theatre aim at posing questions. "What would you do in that situation?", "Where was the point in the history of the protagonist where a shift could have happened, and so the crime would not have been committed?", "What would the

206 Wolf and Baumann (2004): 25 Translated by the author.
207 Wolf and Baumann (2004²): 15 Translated by the author.
208 Wolf and Baumann (2004): 26 Translated by the author.
209 Kuftinec and Alon (2007): 283
210 Hughes in Thompson (1998): 55

protagonist have needed...?", "Which would be an alternative behaviour of the protagonist to fulfil her needs?" Questions like these are common to ask the participants. Hence, it is not surprising that thereby reflection about one's own life takes place.

Discover one's own potential

> The experience made me feel really important, it made me feel for the first time that it wasn't a pub, it was reaching different people from different walks of life. It helped me to start believing in myself because the same reactions were coming from such different faces.[211]

This quote comes from a woman after a successful theatre performance. I imagine that a triumphant performance pushes one's self-esteem enormously. Compliments, clapping hands, a cheering audience and the feeling that she surprised herself with her own inherent, creative potential will certainly be an invaluable memory. I believe that such positive moments contribute to heal the hearts of anyone who doubts her or his unique worthiness. Even though this extraordinary effect might vanish in the future, there will still remain a happy, empowering memory stored inside.

"[M]any people rediscovered that they are much more than their social roles [...] They discovered that they are unique, individually and collectively"[212], Bárbara Santos conveys.

> Even if the society at large will never really believe that someone who killed another person can be redeemed enough to be accepted back into the human community, these men believe that they will find the ways to come to peace with themselves and with those whom they have hurt. [...] Again, this is not to deny what they have done, but it is also to recognize that they are not *only* what they have done.[213]

Michael Bettencourt tells that it is not primarily about changing society's picture of criminals, but of helping them to transform the negative picture they have of

---

211 Gladstone and McLewin in Thompson (2008): 85
212 Santos in Under Pressure (2008): 6
213 Bettencourt (2000): 6

themselves. In the personal conversations that I had with a few former inmates, all of them agreed that when they left the prison they felt that they carried an aura of shame and sore consciousness around them. The negative pictures of themselves, burdened with guilt, in combination with the prejudices and rejection which they as ex-cons face from society contributes largely to the probability of reoffending. Therefore, in any case strengthening the people's trust in themselves and supporting them to regain self-confidence is tremendously important – for the individual inmate as well as for the community in which she or he will return!

Changes in the *here* and *now* - or in the future?

> I have just taken part in a workshop where I have cried, hugged, laughed, played in ways that I have never done in the past. I have changed totally. Perhaps next week I will have unsafe sex. I don't know. Why are you so obsessed with the future? What has happened now is most important.[214]

With these words a participant of an HIV/AIDS theatre workshop in a Brazilian prison summed up his experiences. For the British facilitator Paul Heritage these sentences raised fundamental questions. He wondered whether it is sufficient to test the value of theatre work in some undetermined future by focussing on its social impact. Do we possibly overlook the values of theatre work in the very moment of its process by drifting away too far into the ideal of a better future? How is it determined whether a prison theatre project was successful? Who invents the criteria to measure the usefulness of Theatre of the Oppressed in prison?

In order to get permission to conduct a theatre project in prison –or to be financed– facilitators are forced to explain its profitability. Social skills, teambuilding, rehabilitation, reduction of the re-offending rate or increase of the individual's capability to reintegrate into society are just some of the criteria to determine its utility. Simply having a good time and being momentarily happy would not be enough of a reason to spend money on it, would it?

Is it helpful to force creative work into a cage of analytical usefulness? Acknowledging the importance of rational evaluation of the effects of theatre in pri-

214 Heritage in Balfour (2004): 190

son, I still think that a merely pragmatic focus deprives theatre of its aesthetic magic. I am convinced that there are healing aspects inherent in theatre work, which occur throughout the process and are beyond visible measurement. Michael Balfour criticizes that the

> language used to justify artistic activities in prison becomes functional, for example drama may become 'social skills'; performance may become 'life-skill rehearsals'; the arts are justified as tools of the prison to increase self-esteem and team building – everything must be justified in pragmatic, physical terms.[215]

Theatre of the Oppressed in prisons balances along the paradox of whether it is mainly *useful* – in the sense of creating visible social change – while on the other hand it has a momentary value in itself, apart from its outcome. It is self-evident that the sustainability of its effects ought to be examined, however, it must always be taken into account that the process in itself, and the moments of joy, emotion, closeness and the sensation of inner freedom, that come with it also make a difference. Even though certain effects might be transient, I think that one moment in which the heart is filled with feelings, which are shared with the group, is a big success.

Question and challenge the system

> As prisoners and guards begin to talk about the hidden worlds they inhabit, they can start to participate in public and urgent debates about crime, violence and orisons in ways that challenge the dominant discourses that condemn us all to live in the ever increasing shadows of the borderlands that we have created.[216]

This statement of Heritage expresses the necessity of giving prisoners *and* guards the stage to voice their experiences and their doubts about the criminal justice system. Who, if not the representatives of either side of the iron bars, gets in touch with the prison's inherent contradictions, its problems, its injustice, its violence, and its oppressive conditions? Who, if not prisoners and prison staff, can spark a discussion about dominant discourses by sharing their experiences

---

215 Balfour (2004): 7
216 Heritage in Balfour (2004): 201

with a society who is largely ignorant of prison life? Performances outside the prison especially qualify to address a larger population.

In a unique project conducted in Israel, male prisoners and female students elaborated a play together. The very interesting essence of this collaboration seemed to be the question of "whether the individual or society bears responsibility for oppressive actions."[217] Throughout the nine-month long process "the prisoners acknowledged the need to take responsibility for their actions, but also required the students – as representatives of 'normative society' – to acknowledge various ethnic and racial discriminations that they suffered."[218] Even though the facilitators of this project, Chen Alon and his team, made use of different Theatre of the Oppressed methods, the significant difference was that

> Theatre of the Oppressed typically calls for work with homogenous 'oppressed' groups who Boal calls upon to create alliances with other oppressed groups. Within the prison space, this kind of alliance becomes difficult, in part because of the complexity of identifying either the male prisoners or the female students as 'oppressed'. Yet, through the theatrical process, both groups come to see the other as transformable.[219]

I read in the project's report that the theatre work affected both groups deeply. Prisoners who did not take responsibility for their actions before turned into individuals who acknowledged the responsibility for their deeds. The students on the other hand, were not conscious before about their contribution to a society in which crime happens on a daily basis. Some of them believed that it was only because of their own individual behaviour that they are successful – not due to social structures that support a well-educated middle-class and favour certain thoughts and persons of the establishment. Notably, academics, politicians or entrepreneurs are in power to define crime.

This example is one of several prison theatre projects which, through the means of dialogue between individuals and between different groups, contributed to a critical analysis of social structures and to the realization of individual and collective responsibility. I genuinely appreciate when Theatre of the Oppressed prison projects rise beyond the dualistic categorisation of *oppressor* and *oppressed.* Finding new ways to approach the complexity of oppression by connec-

---

217 Kuftinec and Alon (2007): 281
218 Kuftinec and Alon (2007): 282
219 Kuftinec and Alon (2007): 287

ting different groups –who both have experiences of being oppressed as well as of acting oppressively– is certainly richer in diversity as well as more self-reflective.

WHAT DOES THE PRACTISE LOOK LIKE?

Methods

When Theatre of the Oppressed is applied in prison there are certain methods which are common to use. Generally warm-up games, exercises to become aware of the own body and sensual perception, or trust-games are performed at the beginning of a workshop. Often the second step is to use image theatre to enter into challenging issues. "Our theatre work takes its contents and its energy from the people who participate, from their life experiences and their visions."[220] This quote expresses the approach of Theatre of the Oppressed in which the workshop facilitators do not decide over the topic for a Forum play, but rather it originates from discussions between participants which are sparked by the Image Theatre. Common themes of Forum plays in prisons are for example oppression, in/justice, crime, daily prison life, visions for the life after prison, drugs, physical or psychological violence, domestic and structural violence, peer pressure, dependency on substances, existential/financial dependence on men, the struggle to be separated from one's children, invisibility of prisoner's to the public and various others.[221]

In a next step Forum scenes are developed. This is either done by the usual means of Theatre of the Oppressed or in combination with the *Blagg!* technique. Inspired by Theatre of the Oppressed the TiPP centre in Manchester additionally adopted elements of cognitive behaviour group work and created *Blagg!* "The central element of Blagg! is the creation of a fictional character by a group of offenders. This character is the protagonist of the program and stands for the shared experiences of all group members [...] The life story is exemplary for the biographies of the participants."[222] "The group analyzes the background of the offence and examines its effects on the protagonist and all other people involved,

---

220 Wolf and Baumann (2004): 5
221 Wolf and Baumann (2004), Bettencourt (2000), Matthijssen (2007), Thompson (2000)
222 Opdebeeck in Under Pressure (2008): 14

including the victim(s)."[223] "Blagg! is not meant to replace the current behaviour by a specified other behaviour, but to open up the perspective to many different options of alternative behaviour while simultaneously offering tools to establish pros and cons of any of these options."[224]

This character is called Jo Blagg, or any other name according to the language of the country in which is applied. Many Theatre of the Oppressed practitioners work with this method in prison because projecting one's own experiences, feelings or fears onto Jo Blagg enables participants to feel safe while speaking out openly.

"Forum Theatre gives participants opportunities to rehearse change and acknowledge alternative solutions, but these must be realistic and adaptable."[225] Rehearsing realistic, alternative strategies of conflict resolution is one argument why Forum Theatre is applied to prisons. Another could be that Forum plays are appropriate for performing in front of a wider audience of spect-actors. In this way the issues of the prisoners and the problems of prisons can be communicated to the public. Prisoners and visitors might search for alternatives in a collective process. Apart from Image and Forum Theatre, 'Cop in the Head' and 'Rainbow of Desire' are common techniques to use when working in prison and dealing with internalized oppression or unconscious desires and needs.[226]

As Theatre of the Oppressed practitioners who work in prisons often have a variety of theatre techniques available in their tool-kit it is not surprising that every workshop is unique and enriched with a colourful spectrum of methods. Some work with masks and puppets, as for example *TheaterDialog* in Germany.[227] Roberto Mazzini includes discussing newspaper articles on prisons into the process of creating a Forum Play. Furthermore it is common to do integrative theatre work with prisoners or prisoners on probation together with groups of students, people with learning difficulties, youth or others.

---

223 Matthijssen (2007): 3
224 Matthijssen (2007): 7
225 McCoy and Blood in Balfour (2004): 129
226 See Gladstone and McLewin in Thompson (1998): 80, Bettencourt (2000): 3
227 Famous for working with masks in prison theatre, yet without explicit connection to Theatre of the Oppressed is 'The Geese Theatre Company' in the UK and the USA. See http://www.geese.co.uk/HTML/index.html

Practitioners

I will now mention names of Theatre of the Oppressed practitioners who are or have been actively working in prisons. This selection is reduced to those practitioners who I have either had personal contact with, whose articles I came across during my research or who I have been told of by others members of the Theatre of the Oppressed community. This listing is unique as it draws its information from a variety of prison theatre projects in different parts of the world. All of them openly claim a connection with Theatre of the Oppressed. These sources are an intercultural and transcontinental selection and thereby aim at linking individual practitioners, theatre groups, interesting projects and unique, imaginative ideas together for mutual inspiration. I do not claim that this listing is complete, it is rather an invitation to work together on a network of practitioners who apply Theatre of the Oppressed to prison – it wants to initiate connection!

Bárbara Santos has been working in Brazilian prisons for many years with CTO Rio. James Thompson, Michael Balfour, Paul Heritage and Jenny Hughes worked at TiPP Centre in the UK and have experience with theatre in the prison and probation field in different countries such as in the United States and in Brazil. Till Baumann and Katrin Wolf conducted at least five projects in prison with the theatre group *TheaterDialog*[228] in Sachsen-Anhalt, Germany. Roberto Mazzini and the group *Giolli*[229] have been running theatre workshops in prisons in Northern Italy. Luc Opdebeeck and Ronald Matthijssen work in the Netherlands with the organisation *Formaat*[230] and facilitated workshops in Dutch and German prisons. Ivana Marijancic has conducted at least three prison theatre workshops in Croatia. Hector Aristízabal with the group *ImaginAction*[231] and Michael Bettencourt have experience with prison theatre in the United States of America. Chen Alon conducts community theatre projects with students within prisons in Israel.

Duration

The duration of a Theatre of the Oppressed in prison program varies between a few days workshop up to a nine-month or one year long project. The most usual

---

228 TheaterDialog (2009): http://www.domino-x.de/theaterdialog.htm
229 Giolli (2009): see http://www.giollicoop.it/
230 Formaat (2009): see http://www.formaat.org/inenglish/index.php
231 ImaginAction (2009): see http://imaginaction.org/

time span is around two or three months, with one session per week. I assume that there would be a strong interest from both sides – participants as well as facilitators – to expand the time span, yet it seems to be difficult to get the permission as well as funding for long term projects.

WHAT FREEDOM CAN THERE BE IN PRISON?

Radical Freedom

Of all texts by theatre makers that mention freedom, I have found one that comes close to the definition of freedom in chapter II. Baz Kershaw's idea of *radical freedom* invokes that it

> [...] is not just freedom *from* oppression, repression, exploitation – what we could call the resistant sense of the radical – but also freedom to reach beyond existing systems of formalised power, freedom *to* create currently unimaginable forms of association and action – what I call the transcendent sense of the radical.[232]

Kershaw calls for a transcendent radicalism, which asks about the direction towards which change shall happen. This approach goes along with Osho's critique on merely focussing on the freedom *from*, but instead raising the question of what we want freedom *for*. Kershaw's argument is very refreshing in an environment, which emphasises the importance of resistance. I support his calls for 'creating currently unimaginable forms of association and action'. Theatre of the Oppressed analyses conditions, which are not favourable, such as oppression or injustice, and questions how to *get away from* these situations. Consequently it asks where to go *to* and creates images of an alternative reality.

Nevertheless, it was possibly never explicitly mentioned that when working in prisons, the more constructive questions are: What do they want to do when they get out of the prison? What does somebody want to be (physically) free for? What do we want to create, when we are free from certain hindrances? Otherwise, ignoring these questions any individual might get stuck in reactive resistance

232 Kershaw in Balfour (2004): 36 Italicised by the author.

or angry opposition instead of proactively, creatively and freely taking responsibility for one's own life.

Easier to be in the Here and Now?

The circumstances for the participants of the Theatre of the Oppressed workshops in prison are such that often any break in the routine of prison life is welcome. As Boal explained, there might be freedom in time, where there is no freedom of space. When life seems like one eternal never-ending moment, forced into years of the very same schedules – as suffocative and unbearable as this sounds – there could, however, be the time to quietly look at oneself.

> In prison, I had a certain kind of freedom. We, who are free in space, are prisoners of time. Those who are prisoners of space, of time become free. Outside in the daily routine of life, the day to day tasks would not allow me to see myself – I was in a hurry, always doing, going to do, seeing it done: in my cell, I was obliged to look at myself and see. Outside, schedules, tasks, smiles – the rituals of life gave me no time to reflect. [...] Now that I had time, I had no space. In the diffuse disintegration of time in prison – that time in which now was permanent, no before or afterwards: just the eternal moment existed – and in the concentrated scantiness of the dense space, I thought of myself. There, I heard the sound of silence.[233]

These sentences of Augusto Boal, in which he described his own experiences in prison, raises the question whether the fact of being free in time (which is only partly true as the schedules are strictly decided on by the prison authorities) makes it easier to delve completely into the here and now? It might be cynical to claim that, as I have never been to prison myself, yet I imagine that Boal has a point in saying that being exposed to a never-ending moment of *Now*, deprived of most kinds of distractions, carries a potential which can be destructive as well as enlightening.

These stinted preconditions can be fertile ground for theatre. Michael Bettencourt wrote: "In a space not noted for affection, we all got out of our 'other' skins for a moment and linked spirit to spirit, none of us defined but simply here and fully witnessed."[234] I wonder, whether, as the contrast between the daily rou-

---

233 Boal in Balfour (2004): 194f
234 Bettencourt (2000): 6

tine of prison-life and a colourful theatre process is stronger than between most other circumstances, the effects might even be amplified.

Critical Viewpoints of Theatre of the Oppressed in Prisons

Who is teaching who?

As most Theatre of the Oppressed in prison projects are limited to an average time span of two or three months, they rarely have the explicit goal to train inmates who serve a long-term or life-sentence in theatre methods in a way that they can become capable of facilitating workshops themselves. In fact, experimenting with theatre and the opportunity to explore oneself through creative work is dependant upon whether there are artists who visit the prison, run a workshop and leave after the program has finished.

The CTO Rio however, intends to train multipliers who consequently transfer theatre methods further. In the prison of Papuda in Brazil there exists the "established principle of passing on techniques and processes that others could continue. In Britain most of the work we generate is controlled by the authorities in such a way that little is left but a memory when we leave."[235] In some Brazilian prisons it functions very well that those prisoners who have gained experiences with theatre continue the work by passing on their knowledge to others. In this way, the continuity of theatre work in prison is permitted by the institution on the one hand and facilitated by the commitment of inmates on the other hand.

Continuity of Theatre of the Oppressed in prison work is a further issue. As a major hindrance to establish a permanent and stable theatre group in prison seems to be the lack of finances, I wonder, would it then not be an appropriate option to empower prisoners to create and lead workshops themselves?

The trap of wanting to educate prisoners into 'good citizens'

The challenge for Theatre of the Oppressed practitioners who work in the prison system is to not fall into the trap of wanting to *reform* the inmates. "We always talk about *resocializing criminals.* Why do we never ask how to *decriminalize society*?" [236] This quote of Julian Boal[237] expresses sharply the danger of being

235 Heritage in Thompson (1998): 36f

236 Boal, Julian (2008): Quote taken from his lecture on the 9th of April 2008, at VHS Meidling, Vienna.

incorporated into a mindset which focuses at *re-habilitating, re-forming, re-integrating* the individual prisoner without questioning the social context.

Theatre of the Oppressed has clear ethical principles. Hence, Theatre of the Oppressed practitioners are not immune either – like all other human beings – of falling into the trap of hammering the own values into others, wanting to change them. This might not happen in an obvious way, but very subtly while generously promoting participative theatre – often without them noticing it.

James Thompson wrote a very genuine reflection about his experiences with that trap in the 'Annual Review of Critical Psychology'. He started out admitting that at the beginning of their offending behaviour workshops they assumed that certain forms of behaviour would be automatically seen as problematic by the participants. Surprisingly, "many prisoner groups, particularly young offenders, saw nothing wrong with hitting their partners or stealing cars"[238]. Therefore, Thompson and his colleagues assumed that they would have to show the problematic consequences of certain behaviour, because if there is no necessity for change, none would intervene in Forum scenes.

When Thompson and his group worked in Brazil later on, they realized the problem that "an agenda of change set from the outside is an imposition, not an act of liberation."[239] According to James Thompson much of the rehabilitative group work in the criminal justice system of the UK and the USA "presents a behaviour ideal that the group must reach."[240] The ideal of the good, obedient citizen is targeted. He concluded that "we should not be telling groups what sort of citizens they should be, but involving them in creating their own visions of the way they connect to their society."[241] He describes the potential of prison theatre as a process of learning to be involved in the community, while at the same time scrutinizing it from a critical distance.

> Prisons and probation services seek to create good – well behaved – citizens. Prison theatre practise could become a process of encouraging critical citizenship – providing a point of connection between the prisoner and their communities, but also giving them a voice to critique and change the community. [242]

---

237 Julian Boal is the son of Augusto Boal, forum theatre maker and director of the Paris Theatre of the Oppressed.

238 Thompson (2000): 186

239 Thompson (2000): 188

240 Thompson (2000): 188

241 Thompson (2000): 188

242 Thompson (2000): 189

This is a crucial issue to raise, because there is a fine line along which Theatre of the Oppressed practitioners have to balance if they want to do honest participatory theatre, while obviously being driven by personal and societal values and ideals of what is good or harmful.

It also needs structural changes

"This was such a good group, and now the same shit starts again."[243] These were the concluding words of an adolescent participant in a prison theatre project in Germany. He hit the nail on the head: If a theatre workshop continues for a few weeks it might have certain positive effects on the participants, but these effects might easily be weakened, forgotten and replaced by the frustration of every-day prison life. Theatre certainly has a great potential, but measures ought to go further than being a mere momentary distraction. There is "no point in predicating work on the idea of personal change – as ultimately cognitive behavioural work does – if the extreme conditions of poverty that the vast majority of prisoners come from and return to are not transformed."[244] Referring to a Brazilian context, James Thompson calls for linking personal change to community change. Otherwise theatre in prison cannot contribute to a sustainable, social impact.

Long-term prison theatre projects have the potential to question and transform social structures. For instance, if the relationship between prisoners and prison staff eases and carries increased ability to trust in it, both parties might collaborate to change the atmosphere in prison towards mutual respect and niches of freedom. Consequently, prisoners might be empowered to express their needs more directly.

Another potential of furthering structural change exists when prisoners perform Forum theatre plays outside the prison, as for example at universities or in public places. (However, it is not enough to do that only once, but it needs continuity in addressing and discussing issues with the public.) Society's idea that 'prisons are necessary to protect us from dangerous criminals' can be challenged, by meeting these *dangerous criminals*, getting informed about their experiences before and in prison – and thereby perceiving them as human beings. In this way it might become visible to a greater part of society that prisons in many cases do more harm than they actually help.

---

243 Wolf and Baumann (2004^2): 18
244 Thompson (2000): 187

Why do inmates not comment on effects on them themselves?

"Theatre run by outside practitioners has become more known, whilst the work started and sustained by prisoners themselves is rarely documented."[245] As this is the case in prison theatre projects in general, that lack of documentation from the prisoner's perspectives brings me to a similar question: Theatre of the Oppressed is about giving *the oppressed* a voice. However, the research literature available to find out more about the effects it has on participants of prison theatre has all been documented, with rarely any exception, by workshop facilitators. Of course it is valuable to keep records of the workshop leaders' observations, but this is simply one point of view. Artists, social activists or academics who already have a voice, talk about the experiences of the prisoners – but the prisoners themselves do not write or tell the public about what Theatre of the Oppressed has changed for them. Is that not exactly what Augusto Boal always criticized: that the dominant side speaks on behalf of the so-called oppressed?

Why is it so difficult to find these voices in literature? Is it because after opening up emotionally within the workshop it would be too much of a challenge for participants to communicate their experiences to outsiders? Is it because many prisoners have reading or writing difficulties and therefore hesitate to write a short personal essay about what they learnt, thought and felt throughout the theatre process? By the way, is there any importance in communicating the effects of Theatre of the Oppressed prison workshops to the public? Or is there also an underlying issue of the prisoner's intimacy and sharing the safe workshop space with outsiders would be a too sensitive undertaking?

I do not know. I did not accompany a prison theatre project, nor did I get in touch with inmates who took part themselves. I merely wonder. And I ask you, workshop facilitators and Theatre of the Oppressed community, why is that so? If it is argued that Theatre of the Oppressed has liberating effects on participants, I want to be convinced by statements of the people themselves!

Support in dealing with issues that arise from deep self-reflection

Theatre work frequently brings psychological issues to light. Deep, personal, maybe even traumatic experiences might be remembered, triggered by discussions, role-plays, trusting games or others. Therefore, there ought to be a safe space and qualified personnel to back up the individuals in these moments. Are

245 Thompson (1998): 15

there psychologists, therapists, or group members who will take the time to support other participants in difficult processes? This sensitive point is often dealt with through a close collaboration with prison staff as psychologists, social workers, and therapists.

Conclusion

Theatre of the Oppressed balances along the paradox of on the one hand wanting to enter the penitentiary system in order to transform it from inside – and to reach the prisoners! – while on the other hand being in resistance to a justice system which bases on punishment and on a definition of justice created by an intellectual/political elite. Out of this major paradox a number of challenges arise. The necessity of funds in order to carry out a project and thereby risking a dependence on certain institutions is only one of many.

Theatre of the Oppressed prison projects have already been carried out in Brazil, Great Britain, USA, Germany, Netherlands, Israel, Croatia, Italy and Austria[246] – and possibly others of which I did not find any documentation. The majority of these projects were conducted in the years 2001-2008 and I assume the idea of bringing Theatre of the Oppressed to prisons is spreading. The average time span of such projects is 2-3 months, though there are few which continued for almost one year. Forum theatre and Image theatre are the most common methods of the Theatre of the Oppressed arsenal and they are frequently combined with tools from improvisational theatre, cognitive behaviour theory, mask/puppet theatre among others.

The chapter on Critical Viewpoints expresses the necessity to be careful about certain crucial issues. I frequently came across the question on the sustainability of effects reached by a theatre workshop and I think practitioners and groups can learn a lesson from the approach within the prison of Papuda, Brazil. There, skills, tools and methods are taught to some inmates who are then invited to pass on their experiences to other inmates. Thereby the chance to play theatre, elaborate plays and engage creatively is not totally dependent on artists coming from outside and leaving after a few weeks/months.

Throughout my literature research, I realized once again the enormous challenge to practise genuine Theatre of the Oppressed, which aims at changing opp-

246 In 2005 the group *Interact* from Graz facilitated a 6-session forum theatre project in the Justizanstalt Klagenfurt. See: http://www.interact-online.org/projekte_gruppen_justizanstalt.htm

ressive situations, while at the same time resisting the temptation of forcing one's own truth upon others.

Even though I believe that there is the possibility for moments of freedom, moments of joy and moments of closeness inside the prison, I feel the necessity to express my genuine doubts surrounding the prison system.

Prison Critique

Introduction

Throughout my literature research I came across innumerable points of critique about the prison system. This literature was mainly written by artists and/or social activists. While writing I kept my ears open whenever I heard something about prisons. I talked to Austrian ex-prisoners and guards and listened to their critique. This Prison Critique chapter is intended as an *insertion* which contributes to my main topic, but is not my focus in this book. Instead of delving deeply into the topic of prison critique, I will instead explain my personal impressions about the absurdity of prisons and raise a number of arguments that hopefully provoke both, you as a reader and myself as author.

Consequently, I will raise arguments as well as a few statistic examples from an Austrian context. Even though the United States prison regime would inspire and deserve harsh critique – with more than 2.3 million prisoners, the U.S.A. accounts for 25% of the global prison population while making up only 5% of the world's population[247] – I decided to take Austrian examples as this is the country with which I am most familiar.

A Short-Sighted World-View of Punishment, Revenge and Justice

Prisons *function* because there is a general agreement that there are serious mistakes – sins? – that ought to be atoned for. They can exist because thoughts of revenge and punishment are often the immediate response when it comes to crime related issues. "In the context of prison, this humanising process will never be a fundamental priority [...] Prison is the business of containment, observation, punishment, categorisation, restriction, separation, and on occasion rehabilitation."[248] Prisons aim neither at healing nor at reconciliation. Prisons do not enhan-

247 Join Together (2008)
248 Balfour (2004): 3

ce reintegration of people labelled as criminals into their communities, nor are they institutions, which dig deeply enough to understand the needs or circumstances that have brought individuals to prison. Hence, the personal psychological origins of an alleged criminal, as well as the social and political structures that contribute to crime, are often ignored. Prisons numb the symptoms instead of dealing with or healing the roots of criminal acts. If the major argument is that prisons work because "at least when a man is in prison, he cannot commit any more crimes"[249], it shows the short-sightedness of these institutions.

SOCIETY'S RESPONSIBILITY FOR INDIVIDUAL DEEDS

The question of society's responsibility for the crimes of individuals rarely arises. Crime is generally seen as individual misbehaviour. Criminals are often labelled the *black sheep* in a society of white sheep. I would appreciate an approach to crime in which everyone asks oneself about one's responsibility for a crime committed by somebody else, because it might be true that criminal deeds are simply the shockingly genuine mirrors of our society – the visible peaks of an iceberg whose true enormity is comfortably hidden below the surface.

Why are we surprised that burglary, theft and financial fraud occur so frequently, when our culture identifies so strongly with possession and wealth? Do crimes against personal property originate in a world-view largely defined by *having* rather than by *being*? Is it not self-evident that as soon as we define the value of a person by her reputation or by what she *has*, we force her into longing to become worthy by gaining property?

Furthermore the question arises: Who is committing a property crime? From which social stratum do people who see no other options than to steal and rob others arise? For instance, it is logical that people who have no working permit in a country – to which they have migrated or fled – are more prone to utilise illegal means of raising money for their survival, than those who have the legal right to work.

What motivates violent offences? And to what degree do they result from frustration with unsatisfying, stressful working conditions, broken family backgrounds, sexual discontent or society's incapacity to deal maturely with emotions and aggression? The anonymity engendered by big cities further exacerbates

---

249 Heritage in Balfour (2004): 192

feelings of isolation and loneliness, a general lack of social support networks; just as the myth of the survival of the fittest engenders mutual mistrust and the fear of being left behind. All those factors certainly play a role in criminal offences.

Answering these questions would reach far beyond this research, yet I posed them to express my conviction that society at large *also* bears responsibility for individual criminal acts. However, this is no excuse to neglect the individual responsibility for our deeds. Along the narrow spine of this paradox between social and individual responsibility the question of crime and prisons balances.

THE USUAL SUSPECTS

Who is committing a crime? Or, who goes to prison for committing an act, which is *defined* as crime? Roberto Mazzini, an Italian Theatre of the Oppressed practitioner states that "the ones offending law are the majority of population, but who enter prisons are an *elite* on the contrary: that is people from low social classes, poor, marginalized ones. Today in Italy immigrants, Gypsies, drug-addicts, drop-outs are the majority of prisoners."[250] "Social, economical and racial factors determine global prison population as much as legal and judicial agencies"[251] – Paul Heritage argues.

Angela Davis, a committed prison abolitionist, activist and university professor in the U.S.A. points out: "[...] many people from communities of Afro-Americans, Latinos and Native Americans today have a greater chance to go to prison, than receiving a proper education."[252] Speaking of the racial disparities in U.S. prisons, Human Rights Watch reports on new statistics which show that

> black males [are] incarcerated at a per capita rate six times that of white males. Nearly 11 percent of all black men ages 30 to 34 were behind bars as of June 30, 2007. [...] Although whites, being more numerous, constitute the large majority of drug users, blacks constitute 54 percent of all persons entering state prisons with a new drug offense conviction. [...] black men [are] 11.8 times more likely than white

---

250 Mazzini in Under Pressure (2008): 6
251 Heritage in Balfour (2004): 192
252 Davis (2004): 12 Translated by the author.

> men to enter prison on drug charges, despite the fact that blacks and whites use illegal drugs at similar rates.[253]

Unfortunately, such disproportionate numbers of persons belonging to ethnic and national minorities in the prison population are not only an issue in the U.S.A. but worldwide.

For example, of the total 8600 prisoners in Austria, 3 638 come from more than 100 different nations and do not have Austrian citizenship.[254] This means that almost 43% of all prisoners in Austria are foreign citizens, while they represent only 10.4% of the total population of Austria.[255] These numbers must be read as evidence for racist, discriminatory structures in the criminal justice systems in Austria as well as elsewhere. Stereotypes of black Africans as drug dealers or Eastern Europeans as thieves contribute to innumerable random arrests in the streets of Vienna and create a climate of hostility and fear towards foreign citizens which, consequently, further strengthens the popular perception of them as criminals.

ALMOST 50% OF AUSTRIAN PRISONERS HAVE PENALTIES OF LESS THAN 1 YEAR

Approximately 40% of Austrian prisoners serve sentences between one and five years – and slightly more than 10% are sentenced to more than five years in prison.[256] This sounds like good news at a first glance: 'What a relief! The majority of prisoners are no hard-boiled, brutal murderers and rapists but petty criminals!' However this assumption gives me pause.

If one common argument in favour of prisons is the protection of society from truly dangerous individuals, then why do we not set free at least half of the current prisoners – those who allegedly committed non-violent crimes? Instead of putting those people in prison, thereby creating grave consequences for their permanent record – which might make them even more prone to criminal acts – why not offer non-violent offenders the opportunity to undertake alternative

253 Human Rights Watch (2008)
254 Justizanstalten (2009)
255 Statistics Austria (2009): Population by citizenship and country of birth
256 Jahresbericht (2008): 11

forms of compensation such as reconciliation, mediation, restorative justice or reparation of what has been destroyed?

Another argument against putting petty criminals behind bars is that they will learn more about drugs and crime in prison than possibly anywhere else. A common saying is that prisons are the 'schools of crime'. "Sometimes, an individual entering prison to await trial for a minor offence might return to the community a 'hardened criminal' (more aggressive and prone to violence and crime) [...]"[257]. Although this quote originates from a South African context, it is alarmingly similar to statements of female prisoners in the Austrian documentary film "Gangster Girls"[258]. I think that this is not an extraordinary effect, but inherent in the workings of prisons in many parts of the world.

INSTITUTIONALIZED DEPENDENCE AS PREPARATION TO LIVE RESPONSIBLE LIVES?

What happens after prisoners are released into society? Many of them will return to prison sooner or later. The first obstacle after release will be to find an employer who will give a job to an ex-con. Most former inmates return to their families and friends; hence into the circles where slipping back into the vicious circle of crime is quite likely.

Certain questions arise: In which ways did a person who has spent several years in prison benefit from the time spent there? How does society at large benefit from locking away people from which a majority will return even more frustrated, aggressive, depressed or broken than they were before? Why is it thought to be *rehabilitative* to be put into a distorted, artificial reality such as a prison, where there is rarely the freedom of choice, nor of participation?

Schedules are strict, movement is continually monitored and restricted, there is no space to be alone, and men and women are separated into different buildings. How, I wonder, does a restricted environment like that contribute to the development of taking responsibility for one's own actions? Does prison give the chance to develop alternative ways of dealing with conflicts, with one's own aggression or with the other sex? No, I do not think so. A prison, in the way it is constructed, suppresses these issues.

---

257 Centre for Conflict Resolution in Balfour (2004): 163

258 Gangster Girls: Austrian documentary film from 2008 by Tina Leisch.

CRIME RATE IS DECREASING, YET CALLS FOR BUILDING NEW PRISONS CONTINUE

> The number of judicial convictions in 2008 (38 226) fell by 11.4% (-4 932 cases) in comparison with reporting year 2007. This meant that the number of convictions fell to a historical all-time low. Overall, the number of convictions (based on 1 000 persons legally considered as of the age of criminal responsibility) for 2008 was 5.33, the lowest figures since these statistics were first compiled in 1947. [...]
>
> The number of criminal convictions (33 044) for crimes in contravention of the Austrian Criminal Code showed a fall of 9.4% (-3 438 cases) from 2008 compared with 2007. Broken down by type of offence, there was a decline in nearly all sub-groups. Convictions for offences against life and limb dropped by -5.3%, those against liberty by 15.0%. Relatively strong was also the decline of convictions against property (-9.6%). [259]

Even the Interior Minister in Austria recognized the decrease of crime in all federal states, almost all border districts and in nearly all regional capital cities, by 6% in the first half of the year 2008 compared to the previous year.[260]

Criminal statistics can be easily exploited by politicians and mass media. The crime rate is constantly fluctuating. It decreases or increases depending on which months or years are selected for comparison. Any small increase in offences will be exaggerated in order to manipulate society into fear and provide new arguments to legitimize even more security policies and surveillance strategies. Acknowledging these fluctuations as well as the limitations of statistics in general, the overall trend in Austria is that the crime rate is decreasing.

While this might be interpreted as a flicker of hope for those of us who want to see less people behind prison bars, the disillusionment comes with the following paradox: The Austrian prison industry is planning to construct three new prisons as well as expanding several existing ones. At the moment, the process of architectural competition for these projects is underway. One new prison will be constructed in Vienna, another in Korneuburg, Lower Austria, and the third in Salzburg.[261]

So, while the crime rate is generally decreasing in Austria, the trend to expand the prison regime is prevalent. Come on, we live in the 21st century; it cannot be

---

259 Statistics Austria (2009): Convictions: Judical Criminal Statistics
260 Bundesministerium für Inneres (2008): Kriminalstatistik
261 Justizstrafvollzug (2007)

true that locking errant human beings up is still the most common practise! What a shame, if we praise our society's foresight and yet still cannot think of more humane options than prisons! Huge investments are required to construct more prisons instead of elaborating sustainable, humane alternatives to prisons such as restorative justice, reconciliation, mediation or therapy. Still more healing methods and treatment centres could be developed if we, as a society, would muster up the courage to think creatively about alternatives instead of remaining stuck in the old-fashioned punishment (il)logic!

OH, LAW ALMIGHTY...

Last but not least, I regard it necessary to attack the seeming untouchable authority of the law. Infringement on a certain law might appear to be enough reason to punish someone, without questioning the reasonability of the very law itself. Laws are constantly changing.

Here are three examples: Until 1971, homosexuality was illegal in Austria.[262] Since the 1960s, it has been legal in the Netherlands to squat in "empty houses that have been empty for over a year."[263] (Although a ban on squatting is currently in preparation.) In the last years in Austria, groups that engaged in political activism, NGO's for animal protection and others have frequently been labelled as 'criminal organisations' by §278a of the Austrian law. This paragraph apparently legitimized surveillance and violation of privacy by the executive.

These are just a few examples to show that laws are no unshakable truths, but have always varied greatly between different states and times – influenced by current social needs or economic interests. This constant transformation and inherent arbitrariness of the law also carries the creative potential to elaborate alternative laws and rights than those existing today. This is what *Legislative Theatre* aims at and what I think might be a way out of criminalizing individuals and putting them behind bars in order to avoid confrontation with complicated issues.

262 Graupner (2001): 4
263 Indymedia (2009)

Conclusion

A number of arguments have been touched on and invite further in-depth scrutiny. The essence of this chapter for me is that a shift of perspective is required: The uncritical acceptance of the prison system must come to an end! There are already alternative approaches, which aim at healing and reconciliation. A world-view of punishment and revenge is outdated because it creates vicious circles of more suffering. Instead of encouraging authentic insights and offering support to become stable, compassionate individuals, imprisonment mainly cultivates aggression or intimidated frustration.

Furthermore, prisons often serve to enact ethnic or racial discrimination, as well as to prevent resistance against established political practises by the threat of incarceration. It is time to abandon the belief that prisons exist to protect society and instead realize that they are powerful tools to exercise control over anyone who does not conform.

In the final conclusion of this thesis, I will elaborate upon the question of whether Theatre of the Oppressed actually transforms the sensation of 'inner freedom' for the inmates, even though their circumstances are everything but free.

Final Conclusion

To evaluate in which ways Theatre of the Oppressed transforms the sensation of 'inner freedom' for the prisoners, I will apply some aspects of freedom, which I defined in Chapter II.6.3. I will then close with personal thoughts around the question of freedom *from* or freedom *for/to*.

Taking responsibility for oneself, the group and the society one lives in

Most reports on Theatre of the Oppressed prison projects noted a change in this aspect. Self-reflection about one's own past, the committed crime or (financial) dependencies on certain persons and substances takes place throughout the theatre process. Scenes on these topics or others are acted out and often contribute to being able to see one's own life from a critical distance. By playfully experimenting with alternative strategies in difficult situations, new possible options emerge. Therein, the true scope of choices is revealed. Then, it is the individual who carries the responsibility for the choices she makes – because she is the protagonist in her own life!

Apart from self-responsibility, any theatre process supports a sense of responsibility for the group. In order to get through trusting games safely; to elaborate a play; to cooperate in inventing authentic characters; and to create an atmosphere in which everyone feels comfortable to act in front of others; for all these facets of theatre work it is necessary that everyone feels responsible for the group. Feedback from participants often expressed the enormous mutual support within the group that arose during the workshop sessions.

On a larger scale, Theatre of the Oppressed projects in prison often result in prisoners (sometimes also prison staff) actively involving themselves in public discourse on crime, punishment, the justice system and prison life. This happens through performing forum plays in public places, inviting an audience from outside to forum performances inside the prison, or by passing on theatre methods and personal experiences to others after leaving the prison. Participating in public debates around one's own life circumstances is certainly a way to take responsibility and transform the society one lives in.

Trust in oneself, others and in life

The capability to trust in oneself and in other people is often observed to have changed after working with Theatre of the Oppressed. Participants frequently point out that at the end of a theatre process they were surprised by the courage they showed. Acting in front of others requires self-confidence, risking embarrassment, critique or ridicule. Furthermore, before expressing oneself on stage, there will usually be a long process of exposing oneself to the group by sharing one's emotions, painful experiences, fears, needs, desires and hopes. This is necessary in Theatre of the Oppressed because all topics of the scenes emerge from personal stories. I assume that having the strength to go through such intense moments of sharing one's own *weaknesses* is already a sign of trusting oneself to an extent, which allows being authentic towards others.

In some projects, people of different groups (students/prisoners, prisoners/prison staff, prisoners/youth or others) are working together on creating scenes. Thereby prejudices of the *other* are deconstructed, which is especially valuable if prisoners and prison staff get together. As there is usually an atmosphere of mistrust, averseness or even hatred amongst the prisoners as well as between prisoners and prison staff, a unifying process of collaboration functions well to clear out negative preconceptions and improve the atmosphere in prison.

Another visible facet of trust is that physical closeness increases. Various reports pointed out that as the theatre work proceeded, participants allowed more physical contacts. This has different reasons. On the one hand, theatre is a physical activity and certain scenes involve physical contact – for example if there are scenes of a group of friends, couples, a family and so on. On the other hand, Theatre of the Oppressed workshops usually create connection by encouraging true dialogue in which everyone is (hopefully) listened to. These factors contribute to building trust which is often expressed by physical closeness even after the workshop has finished.

In terms of 'trust in life' it was not possible for me to ascertain this. To find out whether participants after a Theatre of the Oppressed process are more confident than before that *everything will turn out fine*, would definitely need personal conversations with them. Trusting that every state of mind, every mood will go by, change or vanish and hence, welcoming life's up's and down's, is an attitude that I regard as too far to be reached with a few sessions of Theatre of the Oppressed. Sustaining this attitude is a never-ending challenge for me, who has lived all my life outside of prison, and I will certainly keep on working on it for many more years. So, to develop a deeply rooted trust in life for people who possibly underwent traumatic experiences, abuse and violence, would take a much more profound and long-term process, or a therapy. Still, I think that a

Theatre of the Oppressed program that runs for many months or even a whole year has the potential to make at least slight changes in the capability to 'trust in life'.

Critical *Thinking*

Critical thinking involves becoming aware of oppressive situations and discriminating, social structures. The impression I got from most reports is that the capability of critical thinking transforms visibly. In the dialogues, which precede the elaboration of theatrical scenes certain common issues are identified. Through discussion, the participants often realize that what they thought was their unique, personal problem is actually a wide-spread, common problem for more men and women than they assumed. From that realization it is easy to draw certain conclusions about the society they live in as well as about structures, which favour the development of these problems.

As mentioned before, prisoners who participate in Theatre of the Oppressed projects might enter public debates and make their voices heard more easily. Those who have to live in prison are the ones who can speak out against the conditions in it most strongly, because they talk from their own experiences.

I also observed by reading the reports that changes in both directions occurred at the same time. Participants took more responsibility for their individual deeds while on the other hand, they started criticizing a system in which some parts of society are very likely to get locked up, while other parts of society are more or less immune to ever being confined. (Furthermore, it is a question of unequal opportunities and unfair distribution of goods that contributes to the vicious cycle of criminality.) I see that the process of critical reflection on social circumstances is sparked by Theatre of the Oppressed methods and finds its expression in forum-plays and the subsequent discussion with the spect-actresses.

Self-confidence *and being aware of one's own value – hence daring to be oneself*

Any theatrical work needs the commitment of each individual. Everyone is valuable and contributes in his own, unique way to the outcome of the process. Very generally said, any play performed by a Theatre of the Oppressed prison project is a success. People who never acted before turn out to be great actors; the interactive exchange with the audience is new to most who attend the performance; stories and scenes are thrilling and touching because they show personal experiences; and, if the content of the play truly evolved from the group, a uniting feeling of group-success arises. The impression I got from reading the reports is that a Theatre of the Oppressed (forum) play is somehow prone to be successful, because it is a positive and totally new experience for everyone who participates. (Of course it might be the case that unsuccessful projects exist but are not documented, or that such ineffective aspects of the work are kept quiet!)

In any way, I think that a favourable experience – such as a praised performance – contributes to the individual's feeling of self-confidence. Some participants reported that they have never felt as proud as after the performance. Often family, relatives and friends sit in the audience and compliment them on their acting after the show. I observed that the feeling of having an audience who attentively listens to the group's invented story, which metaphorically voices their collective experiences, contributes to developing self-confidence. Apart from the performance, in the whole workshop process a safe environment is created where everyone can share one's story and is listened to – hence, everyone is important, valuable and given attention.

Furthermore, all reports mentioned how throughout the process participants gradually put off their masks and showed themselves to the group. Hugging, laughing, crying, touching, sharing one's hopes for the future, one's regrets from the past, disclosing the wounds of their hearts and their yearning for love – and after all, still being respected and liked by the group.

Whenever one genuinely opens himself and sees that the others still value him – maybe even more because of his authenticity – I believe that such an experience profoundly affects his ability to be himself.

Not relying more on outer authorities than on one's own experiences

This aspect of freedom is one that Krishnamurti, Osho, Freire and Boal agree on. I observed that especially in forum theatre this could be experienced. The participants and the spect-actors realize that they have a range of good alternatives in their minds and that there is no need for experts to solve the problems that they deal with in their lives. Additionally, they themselves decide whether an alternative idea, posed by an intervention of a spect-actress was enriching, useful or not helpful at all. There is no objectively good or bad solution.

However, I do not dare to affirm that most participants of a Theatre of the Oppressed prison program, from that experience onwards, rely more on their own perceptions than on outer authorities. It might go in that direction. Again, I think it would take long-term programs to facilitate more profound transformation in this regard.

Additional aspects of freedom in which changes have been noted

Trying something new and thereby becoming free of one's conditionings. This aspect has also been occasionally mentioned. Stepping into roles, which are different from one's own identity opens up a new horizon of perspectives and possibilities. Another thing is that many exercises require being fully present in the very moment in oneself, in one's own body, in the group and in the process. The freedom to communicate and express one's feelings, thoughts and ideas is encouraged and visibly increased through Theatre of the Oppressed work.

Changes in all those aspects have been pointed out in different reports and evaluations. For this reason I conclude that Theatre of the Oppressed does actually transform the sensation of inner freedom for the participants. In general, most come out of the process stronger than before and enriched by learning a language to express their needs. I assume that most participants discovered that there are always alternatives in difficult situations and that it is their responsibility, which they choose. Nevertheless, their individual responsibility is only one side of the coin. The other is the responsibility of society for all of its members!

In my research, I focused on the sensation of freedom *within* prison, because I wondered whether freedom can exist in circumstances that I consider the most difficult. From the very beginning, Osho's distinction between *freedom from* and *freedom for/to* has fascinated me. Augusto Boal narrated that when he was in prison he had a certain kind of freedom.[264] He was free in time, yet unfree in space – contrary to his life outside the prison. Boal used his custody as a chance to see himself in a way that he never could before, due to lack of time. He took the time to reflect on his life. It seemed that even when imprisoned he managed to focus on the freedoms he had there, although he could as well have been broken by the lack of freedoms which were multiple. He concentrated on the freedom *to* genuinely look at himself and on the freedom *to* imagine theatre methods and alternative political strategies that he might apply after his sentence. Altogether, he focused on the freedom *to* create instead of merely bemoaning the lack of physical freedom.

It might be that he had the strength for this attitude because he was a political prisoner who, according to him, was granted the freedom to educate himself whereas common prisoners were chained up in their cells. It might as well be

264 See Boal in Balfour (2004): 194f

because he had a strong vision in his heart that kept him going. Or, he was clear what he was fighting for, knowing that he was not alone in that struggle. Whatever it was that encouraged him to think of his freedom *to* create something while being physically unfree, it might be that this attitude is an exception.

> [...] for the lads the drama may have been mostly creating a 'freedom from' existing discipline, authority and so on, but hardly at all dealing with 'freedom to' construct an alternative. In other words, their drama may have been working more in terms of resistant than transcendent radicalism.[265]

This quote from Baz Kershaw expresses that most inmates enjoy the rebellious 'freedom from' aspect of theatre without being aware of its potential to practise the freedom *to* design alternatives. For me, the question arises whether my urge to perceive custody as a chance to experience the freedom of time for self-reflection and invention of alternatives, is a romantic concept, too far from the reality of most prisoners.

Can *outsiders* as artists, theatre practitioners, social activists or academics, who never or only briefly visit a prison, without ever having to live inside one for several years, actually judge it if there is more interest in resisting than in creating? If a person has no prospects in the near future of creating even her own daily life, whereas resistance can be practised on a daily basis in prison, who am I to claim that the freedom *to* create is more satisfying than merely the freedom *from* negative circumstances?

On the other hand, and this is what my research has proved, even a small fissure in daily prison life which encourages people to create alternative images of situations in their lives, sparks a flame of freedom. Discovering creative tools to express themselves contributed to a freedom – what Osho might call *psychological* freedom – that will remain in the hearts of those who participated, even though their bodies remain captured behind bars. Fulfilling hearts with a spark of freedom while being imprisoned is beautiful, it is great! At the same time, there is more that ought to be done: creating alternatives to prisons, because locking away human beings, excluding them from the community as a punishment only leads to more suffering! Merely putting them behind bars, into a *fake* reality where they are patronized and cannot practise alternatives way of interacting

---

265 Kershaw in Balfour (2004): 39

with one another does not prepare them to enter back into society after years of isolation!

Convinced by the potential of applying Theatre of the Oppressed to prisons I close with an optimistic quote of Augusto Boal that might inspire further thoughts.

> In the magic alchemy of art and social life, theatre and prison
> – both limited in time and space – can become synonyms of freedom.[266]

266 Boal (2001): 298

EPILOGUE

When I received the message that this book could be published, I immediately felt that I would need the feedback of those eight friends, who are my most important *muses* and critics in life, in order to feel encouraged to spread it to a wider audience.

Their feedback was incredibly enriching and opened my eyes to facets that I had missed. They brought up new issues and new approaches and the spectrum of possibilities for revision became too broad for me to manage. I had to accept that I could not elaborate all their inspiring thoughts in depth – as this would mean months or years of more work on this book. And even then, it would lack more than it covers. (This is the problem of life, I guess, there will always be more that I do not know, that I cannot do or that I will not experience.) However, I want to share the probably most striking and inspiring feedback with you in this epilogue. Thereby these last pages might become the beginning of a new endeavour, starting out with an aspect of freedom that I overlooked.

Experiencing Freedom *with* others

For some reasons, without being conscious of it, I have put my focus on individual freedom. Krishnamurti's and Osho's approaches to freedom deal with the individual and one's courage to be oneself, to create, or to become inwardly free from outer restrictive structures and norms. The entity who is responsible to develop freedom *from* and freedom *for* is the individual.

This, however, is only one side of the coin. My friend Joschi Sedlak reminded me that there is also the freedom felt when one is *with* somebody else. Freedom then ceases to be a merely individual sensation and arises when two or more people are together – inspiring each other to grow beyond themselves. One might become more open, authentic, playful and creative when she is in communication with a counterpart. Freedom can arise through *relationship*. Freedom can be more than independence from outer circumstances. It is rather to delve into and flow with the outer circumstances. Two people or a group can create an atmosphere of trust and critical thinking – freedom – which is much more difficult to create all by oneself. There is an enormous value, an incredible potential in thinking and living on a collective level!

Freedom does not arise when one is depending on others, convinced that he could never feel free all by himself. However, experiencing freedom together does not automatically mean to be dependent. Dancing is a good metaphor. When two or more people dance together, horizons of movement-possibilities open up, that one would hardly have access to when dancing alone. Yet, this does not mean that either dancer depends on the other in order to be able to dance. In any moment one can step out of the common dance, change the rhythm, change the pace and the movement – dancing alone and still feel free! Or dancing in community and feeling free *and* inspired…

I certainly gave too little attention to the collective level when dealing with freedom. Therefore, I encourage you – and myself – to integrate this new aspect into any freedom concept that we might consider.

THANK YOU...

Petra and Ernst Buchleitner I thank you that you, as my parents, have always supported me on my way up to now. You have given me roots to feel grounded, knowing that I can always come home – and wings to fly to new adventoures. Oma and Marc, thank you for being there in your kind way. Christian, thank you that I constantly learn from you how to love people the way they are. Thank you for our love and your support in any aspect of life. Lisa, thank you that I can be full of trust that our friendship knows no boundaries, neither of time and space nor of our own personal transformations – it keeps on being ever fresh and inspiring. Maria, Suse, Joschi, thank you for being my teachers in terms of trying to keep balance between trust and critical thinking, between celebrating the joy of this magical life and the courage of resistance. Thank you for our friendship.

Norbert Koppensteiner, thank you for your straightforward feedback and your critical, helpful scrutiny. Honestly, you have been the *midwife* of this book!

Thank you, Melinda Lies, for carefully looking through my English spellings. As Norbert has been the *midwife* of this book-project, you have certainly been the *doctor* thoroughly checking its health. I thank you enormously! Thank you, Eden Trenor, for being a source of inspiration, a sister and my last-minute editor.

Thank you, Wolfgang Dietrich, for initiating this highly energetic, uniquely challenging and extraordinary MA Peacestudies program, through which I grew so much. Thank you all the peacenics, my colleagues and friends around the world with whom I will forever be connected. I keep you all in my heart in your individual uniqueness!Thank you, Elisabeth Rohrmoser, Peter Tappler and Renato Szeifert for your honest and profound feedbacks to this current work. Thank you for making me aware of aspects that I have missed. Thank you, Theatre of the Oppressed community and all the theatre practitioners around the globe that have been helpful to me by giving me literature tipps and sharing their thoughts via e-mail, skype or personal conversation with me. Thank you, Michael Balfour for your introductory words, your encouragement and for the work you do! Thank you, to all the people in the ARGE SeniorInnenheim, an old people's home in Vienna, for your authenticity and your humour that always succeeded to bring me back to the ground after the excessive intellectual, brainy activities that have been necessary for this book. Gracias del corazon, a toda la banda de Oaxaca que me dejo experimentar facilitando talleres, por la inspiración que siempre fueron ustedes para mi, por la amistad y la lucha con las herramientas de creatividad que compartimos.Thanks, more than anything, to life itself that it is so generous to host me, providing me with everything that I *really* need and new learning opportunities on every step.

BIBLIOGRAPHY

Bibliography of Books

BABBAGE, FRANCIS (2004): *Augusto Boal*, Abingdon, Oxon, Routledge.
BALFOUR, MICHAEL (2004): *Theatre in Prison - Theory and Practice*, Bristol, Intellect Books.
BOAL, AUGUSTO (2007): *Theatre of the Oppressed*, New York, Theatre Communications Group [First English edition in 1979].
BOAL, AUGUSTO (2006): *Der Regenbogen der Wünsche*, Uckerland, Schibri Verlag [First edition in English 1995].
BOAL, AUGUSTO (2006): *The Aesthetics of the Oppressed*, Abingdon, Oxon, Routledge.
BOAL, AUGUSTO (2001): *Hamlet and the Baker's Son – My Life in Theatre and Politics*, London, Routledge.
BOAL, AUGUSTO (1998): *The Rainbow of Desire – The Boal Method of Theatre and Therapy*, London, Routledge [First published in 1995].
BOAL, AUGUSTO (1992): *Games for Actors and Non-Actors*, London, Routledge.
BOAL, AUGUSTO (1989): *Theater der Unterdrückten – Übungen und Spiele für Schauspieler und Nicht-Schauspieler*, Frankfurt am Main, Suhrkamp Verlag.
DAVIS, ANGELA Y. (2004): *Eine Gesellschaft ohne Gefängnisse? Der gefängnisindustrielle Komplex der USA.* Berlin, Schwarzerfreitag Publishing.
DIAMOND, DAVID (2007): *Theatre for Living – the art and science of community-based dialogue*, Victoria, BC Canada, Trafford Publishing.
DIETRICH, WOLFGANG (2008): *Variationen über die vielen Frieden – Band 1: Deutungen*, Wiesbaden, VS Verlag für Sozialwissenschaften.
DUDEN – DAS HERKUNFTSWÖRTERBUCH (2007): Etymologie der deutschen Sprache; Band 7; 4. Auflage; Mannheim Dudenverlag, Bibliografisches Institut & F.A. Brockhaus AG.
DUDEN – DAS GROßE WÖRTERBUCH DER DEUTSCHEN SPRACHE (1999): Band 6; 3. Auflage; Mannheim Dudenverlag, Bibliografisches Institut & F.A. Brockhaus AG.
WAHRIG - DEUTSCHES WÖRTERBUCH (2006): Hrsg.: Renate Wahrig-Burfeind; 8. Auflage; Gütersloh/München, Wissen Media Verlag, Wahrig.
ETYMOLOGISCHES WÖRTERBUCH DES ALTHOCHDEUTSCHEN (2007): Band III; von Albert L. Lloyd und Rosemarie Lühr u.a.; Göttingen, Vendenhoeck & Ruprecht Verlag.

ETYMOLOGISCHES WÖRTERBUCH DES DEUTSCHEN(2005): Wolfgang Pfeifer u. a.; 8. Auflage; München, Deutscher Taschenbuch Verlag.

FREIRE, PAULO (1996): *Pedagogy of the Oppressed*, London, Penguin Books [First edition in 1970].

FREY, BARBARA (1989): *Theater der Unterdrückten in Europa*, Berlin, Magisterarbeit, Fachbereich Kommunikationswissenschaften an der Freien Universität Berlin.

KRISHNAMURTI , JIDDU (2006): *Das Wesentliche ist einfach – Antworten auf Fragen des Lebens*, Freiburg, Herder Verlag.

KRISHNAMURTI, JIDDU (2003): *Vollkommene Freitheit – Das große Krishnamurti Buch,* Frankfurt am Main, Fischer Taschenbuch Verlag [First edition in 1999].

KRISHNAMURTI, JIDDU (1969): *Freedom from the Known*, New York, HarperCollins Publishers.

ODIERNA, SIMONE AND LETSCH, FRITZ (ED.)(2006): *Theater macht Politik – Forumtheater nach Augusto Boal,* Neu-Ulm, AG SPAK Bücher.

OSHO (2004): *freedom – The Courage to Be Yourself,* New York, St. Martin's Griffin Press.

RIED, STEFAN (2007): *Richtiges (Er-)Leben im Falschen? Versuche zu Augusto Boals Theater der Unterdrückten als Praxis wider die Verdinglichungstendenz der bürgerlichen Gesellschaft*, Diplomarbeit, Universität Wien.

THOMPSON, JAMES (1998): *Prison Theatre- Perspectives and Practices*, London, Jessica Kingsley Publishers.

Bibliography of Internet Sources

BALFOUR, MICHAEL (2009): "The politics of intention: looking for a theatre of little changes",
Griffith University, Australia. Article has been privately sent to me and will appear in the next edition of Research in Drama Education. Available at http://www.informaworld.com/smpp/title~content=t713443379, retrieved on 20/05/2009.
BAUMANN, TILL (2003): "Vom Boden unter der Telefonzelle – Gespräch mit Mitgliedern des 'Zentrums des Theaters der Unterdrückten' in Rio de Janeiro (CTO-Rio)", available at http://www.ila-web.de/theaterszene/274bras_cto_rio.htm, retrieved on 06/05/2009.
BERNIE'S HOME PAGE: "Krishnamurti", available at http://bernie.cncfamily.com/k_pathless.htm, retrieved on 14/04/2009.
BETTENCOURT, MICHAEL (2000): "Theatre of the Oppressed with the Oppressed", Michael Bettencourt, available at http://www.m-bettencourt.com/thoughts/boal.html, retrieved on 28/03/2008.
BLAGG (2003): "The impact of Blagg on challenging and reducing offending by young people. An evaluation of a drama based offending behaviour workshop." Commissioned by Manchester & Bury Youth Offending Teams and TiPP. Centre for Applied Theatre Research, available at Theatre of the Oppressed
http://www.theatreoftheoppressed.org/uploads/library/evaluations/Blagg%20Evaluation%20Report.pdf, retrieved on 02/05/2008.
boal, augusto (2004): "Tree of the Theatre of the Oppressed", Theatre of the Oppressed available at
http://www.theatreoftheoppressed.org/en/index.php?nodeID=3, retrieved on 22/02/2009.
BUNDESMINISTERIUM FÜR INNERES (2008): "Kriminalstatistik – Halbjahresstatistik 2008",
http://www.bmi.gv.at/cms/BK/publikationen/krim_statistik/files/2008/krimstat_Halbjahr_08.pdf, retrieved on 27/10/2009.
GIBRAN, KHALID (2008): "On Freedom", The Prophet [First edition in English 1923]
available at Poet Seers
http://www.poetseers.org/themes/poems_about_freedom
on 15/05/2009.
GLOBAL DIALOGUE SERIES (2008): "Understanding Social Justice through Experience", available at http://global.wisc.edu/dialogue/archive/2007-2008.htm, retrieved on 26/02/2009.
GRAUPNER, HELMUT (2001): „Homosexualität und Strafrecht in Österreich – Eine Übersicht",

Rechtskomitee Lambda, 8. Auflage, Wien. Available at http://www.rklambda.at/dokumente/publikationen/209-9_18082003.pdf, retrieved on 28/10/2009.

HUMAN RIGHTS WATCH (2008): "US: Prison Numbers Hit New High – Blacks Hardest Hit by Incarceration Policy", June 5th 2008, http://www.hrw.org/en/news/2008/06/05/us-prison-numbers-hit-new-high, retrieved on 25/10/2009.

INDYMEDIA (2009): "Squatting ban in the Netherlands approaching", 23.October 2009, available at http://www.indymedia.org/or/2009/10/930398.shtml, retrieved on 28/10/2009.

JAHRESBERICHT (2008): http://strafvollzug.justiz.gv.at/_downloads/Jahresbericht_2008.pdf, retrieved on 24/10/2009.

JOIN TOGETHER (2008): "U.S. Holds a Quarter of All Prisoners Worldwide, Study Says", April 23, 2008, available at, 'Join Together - From the National Centre on Addiction and Substance Abuse at Columbia University', http://www.jointogether.org/news/headlines/inthenews/2008/us-holds-prisoners.html, retrieved on 27/10/2009.

JUSTIZANSTALTEN (2009): "Strafvollzug in Österreich" http://strafvollzug.justiz.gv.at/, retrieved on 24/10/2009.

JUSTIZSTRAFVOLLZUG (2007): "Übersicht über den Strafvollzug im Jahre 2007", http://strafvollzug.justiz.gv.at/_downloads/EndfassungUebersicht2007.pdf, retrieved on 27/10/2009.

KATINKA HESSELINK: "The Life of Jiddu Krishnamurti", available at http://www.katinkahesselink.net/kr/biography.html, retrieved on 12/12/2008.

KUFTINEC, SONJA AND ALON, CHEN (2007): "Prose and cons: theatrical encounters with students and prisoners in Ma'asiyahu, Israel", in *Research in Drama Education: The Journal of Applied Theatre and Performance*, Volume 12, Issue 3, (November 2007), London, Routledge, available at http://www.informaworld.com/smpp/content~db=all?content=10.1080/13569780701559927, retrieved on 08/05/2009.

MARIJANCIC, IVANA (2008): "Few Forum Theatre workshops in Croation prisons" in *Under Pressure- Theatre of the Oppressed International Newsletter*, Year 9, Volume 27 (January 2008), published by ITO available at http://www.theatreoftheoppressed.org/uploads//UP%2027.pdf, retrieved on 07/05/2009.

MATTHIJSSEN, RONALD (2007): "Blagg! Transitions in Prison. The final report of a bi-national pilot of a Participatory Drama program for female offenders in two prisons" available at http://www.zubilis.de/publikationen/publikationen_docs/2.39.03-2007_09_11_Blagg_final_Report2007_mit_Vorblatt_def.pdf, retrieved on 09/05/2009.

MAZZINI, ROBERTO (2008): "Prison, oppressive world, can be a place of liberation?" in *Under Pressure- Theatre of the Oppressed International Newsletter*, Year 9, Volume 27 (January 2008), published by ITO available at http://www.theatreoftheoppressed.org/uploads//UP%2027.pdf, retrieved on 09/05/2009.

OPDEBEECK, LUC (2008): "Working in Women's Prisons in the Netherlands and Europe" in *Under Pressure- Theatre of the Oppressed International Newsletter*, Year 9, Vol. 27 (January 2008), published by ITO available at http://www.theatreoftheoppressed.org/uploads//UP%2027.pdf, retrieved on 07/05/2009.

OSHO (2007): "Books I have loved", available at http://www.osho.nl/New-Osho-NL/EnglBooks/BooksIHave.htm, retrieved on 10/12/2008.

OSHO WORLD (1986): "Death of the mystic J. Krishnamurti", Osho's tribute, available at http://www.oshoworld.com/biography/innercontent.asp?FileName=biography9/09-09-krishnamurti.txt, retrieved on 27/11/2008.

SANTOS, BÁRBARA (2008): "Humanizing Humanity – Theatre of the Oppressed in Prisons" in *Under Pressure- Theatre of the Oppressed International Newsletter*, Year 9, Vol. 27 (January 2008), published by ITO available at http://www.theatreoftheoppressed.org/uploads//UP%2027.pdf, retrieved on 07/05/2009.

SOCRATES ON WASHINGTON STATE UNIVERSITY (1996): Greek Philosophy – Socrates, available at http://www.wsu.edu/~dee/GREECE/SOCRATES.HTM, retrieved on 06/04/2009.

STATISTICS AUSTRIA (2009): "Convictions: Judical Criminal Statistics" http://www.statistik.at/web_en/statistics/social_statistics/criminality/convictions_judicial_criminal_statistics/index.html, retrieved on 27/10/2009.

STATISTICS AUSTRIA (2009): "Population by citizenship and country of birth" http://www.statistik.at/web_en/statistics/population/population_change_by_demographic_characteristics/population_by_citizenship_and_country_of_birth/index.html, retrieved on 25/10/2009.

THEATRE OF THE OPPRESSED (2009): "Prison Theatre", available at http://www.theatreoftheoppressed.org/en/index.php?nodeID=92, retrieved on 05/05/2009.

THEATRE OF THE OPPRESSED (2008): “Evaluations & Reports”, available at http://www.theatreoftheoppressed.org/en/index.php?nodeID=45, retrieved on 26/02/2009.

THEATRE OF THE OPPRESSED (2008): “Yellow Pages”, available at http://www.theatreoftheoppressed.org/en/index.php?nodeID=2, retrieved on 25/02/2009.

THEATRE OF THE OPPRESSED (2009): Condolences by Adrian Jackson, available at http://www.theatreoftheoppressed.org/en/index.php?useFlash=0, retrieved on 19/05/2009.

THOMPSON, JAMES (2000): “Critical citizenship: Boal, Brazil and theatre in prisons”, in *Annual Review of Critical Psychology*, Vol.2, available at http://www.discourseunit.com/arcp/arcp2/ARCP2%20Thompson%20181-191.doc, retrieved on 05/05/2009.

TIPP: “TiPP History”, available at http://www.tipp.org.uk/tipp/index.php?page=history, retrieved on 05/05/2009.

UNDER PRESSURE (2006): Available at http://www.theatreoftheoppressed.org/en/index.php?nodeID=21, retrieved on 18/05/2009.

UNDER PRESSURE (2008): *Under Pressure- Theatre of the Oppressed International Newsletter*, Year 9, Volume 27, January 2008, published by ITO available at http://www.theatreoftheoppressed.org/uploads//UP%2027.pdf, retrieved on 17/05/2009.

WOLF, KATRIN, BAUMANN, TILL AND OTHERS(2004): „Es ist einfach mal schön, frei zu sein im Knast!“, Dokumentation des theaterpädagogischen Projekts „Hauptdarsteller im eigenen Leben“ des Netzwerks TheaterDialog in der Jugenanstalt Raßnitz. Available at http://www.tillbaumann.de/pdf/rassnitz.pdf, retrieved on 01/06/2008.

WOLF, KATRIN, BAUMANN, TILL AND OTHERS(2004[2]): „Hauptdarsteller im eigenen Leben II“, Halle/Berlin, available at http://www.domino-x.de/, retrieved on 01/06/2008.

Bibliography of Foreword by Michael Balfour

COLLINS, CECIL (1947): *The Vision of the Fool*, London, Grey Walls Press.
JACKSON, ANTHONY (2008): *Theatre, Education and the Making of Meanings: Art or Instrument?* Manchester, University of Manchester Press.
SCHONMANN, SHIFRA. (2005): "“Master” versus “Servant”: Contradictions in Drama and Theatre Education" in *Journal of Aesthetic Education*, Vol.39, No.4, Winter: pp.31-39.
SOMERS, JOHN (2006): "Introduction", in *Drama as Social Intervention* by Balfour, Michael and Somers, John, Concord, Captus University Press.

Quotes from Cover Page and Preface

"And I say to you that not a single person is born in the world who has not a certain capacity which will make him proud, who is not pregnant with something to produce, to give birth to something new and beautiful, to make the existence richer. There is not a single person who has come into the world empty" by Osho. Osho (2004): 162

"Mine is the art of inspiring people to turn themselves inside out, transform their suffering into art, their art into awareness and their awareness into action" by Gabrielle Roth.
See http://www.gabrielleroth.com/ retrieved on 5th June 2009.

Further Reading Material

To continue reading on Theatre in Prison or related topics I include a detailed book list, thoroughly elaborated by the TiPP Centre in the UK. [267]

Tools and Games

Baim, C. & Brookes, S. & Mountford, A. (2002) The Geese Theatre Handbook: Drama with Offenders and People at Risk Waterside Press

Bergman, J. and Hewish, S. (2003) Challenging Experience: An Experiential Approach to the Treatment of Serious Offenders Oklahoma City: Wood 'n' Barnes

Bernardi, P. (1992) Improvisation Starters Betterway Books

Boal, A. (1995) Rainbow of Desire London: Routledge

Boal, A. (1992) Games for Actors and Non-Actors London: Routledge

Brandes, D. & Phillips, H. (1979) The Gamester's Handbook Hutchinson

Fine, N. & Macbeth, F. (1992) Playing with Fire Youth Work Press

Johnston, C. (1998) House of Games Nick Hern

Johnstone, K. (1981) Impro London: Methuen

Poulter, C. (1987) Playing the Game 1 & 2 Macmillan

Rohd, M. (1998) Hope is Vital - Theatre for Community, Conflict & Dialogue Portsmouth NH: Heinemann

Prison Theatre

Balfour, M. (ed) (2004) Theatre in Prison - Theory and Practice Bristol: Intellect Books

Gladstone, P. & McLewin, A. (2000) Arts on the Out - The On Road Guide to Arts Opportunities for Ex-Offenders Canterbury: The Unit for the Arts and Offenders Publications

Kershaw, B. (1998) Pathologies of Hope in Drama and Theatre. Research In Drama Education Vol. 3, No. 1

Peaker, A. (2000) Handbook for Artists - A Practical Guide to Working in Prisons Canterbury: The Unit for the Arts and Offenders Publications

Scott Douglass, A. (2007) Shakespeare Inside: The Bard Behind Bars Continuum International Publishing Group Ltd.

---

267 TiPP: Further Reading

Tannenbaum, J. (2000) Disguised as Poem - My Years Teaching Poetry at San Quentin University Press Boston
Thompson, J. (2000) Critical Citizenship: Boal, Brazil and Theatre in Prisons Annual Review of Critical Psychology 2000
Thompson, J. (1998) Theatre and Offender Rehabilitation: Observations from the USA Research In Drama Education. Vol. 3, No. 2
Thompson, J. (1999) Drama Workshops for Anger Management and Offending Behaviour London: Jessica Kingsley Publishers
Thompson, J. (ed) (1998) Prison Theatre: Perspectives and Practices London: Jessica Kingsley Publishers
Williams, Rachel Marie-Crane (ed) (2003) Teaching the Arts Behind Bars Northeastern University Press Boston

General

Boal, A. (1999) Legislative Theatre Routledge
Boal, A. (1972) Theatre of the Oppressed London: Pluto Press
Cohen-Cruz, J. & Schutzman, M. (1994) Playing Boal: Theatre, Therapy, Activism London: Routledge
Department of Culture, Media and Sport (1999) Policy Action Team 10: A Report to the Social Exclusion Unit: Arts and Sport
Goldstein, A. (1999) The Prepare Curriculum - Teaching Prosocial Competencies Research Press, Illinois, USA
Jackson, A. (ed) (1994) Theatre in Education London: Routledge
Jennings, S. (1986) Creative Drama in Groupwork Winslow Press
Johnston, C (2006) The Improvisation Game Nick Hern Books
Kershaw, B. (1999) The Radical in Performance London: Routledge
Kuziakina, N. (1995) Theatre in the Solovki Prison Camp Harwood Academic Publishers
MacDougall, J. & Yoder, P. S. (1998) Contaminating Theatre: Intersections of Theatre, Therapy and Public Health Northwestern University Press
Matarasso, F. (1997) Use or Ornament? The Social Impact of Participation in the Arts Comedia
O'Toole, J. (1992) The Process of Drama London: Routledge
Oddey, A. (1994) Devising Theatre London: Routledge
Read, A. (1993) Theatre and Everyday Life London: Routledge
Somers, J. (ed) (1996) Drama & Theatre in Education: Contemporary Research North York, Ont.: Captus Press
Taylor, P. ed (1996) Researching Drama & Arts Education: Paradigms & Possibilities London: Falmer Press
Winston, J. (1998) Drama, Narrative and Moral Education London: Falmer Press

Criminal Justice

Christie, N. (1994) Crime Control as Industry London: Routledge
Curran & Renzetti (eds) (1994) Theories of Crime Allyn and Bacon
Downes, D. & Rock, P. (1988) Understanding Deviance Clarendon
Foucault, M. (1977) Discipline and Punish London: Penguin
Garland, D. (1990) Punishment and Modern Society Oxford: Clarendon
Graef, R. (1993) Living Dangerously. Young Offenders in their Own Words Harper Collins
Hollin, C. (1990) Cognitive-Behavioural Interventions with Young Offenders Pergamon Press
Matthews & Young, J. (eds) (1989) Confronting Crime Sage Publishers
Mawby & Gill (1987) Crime Victims Tavistock
McGuire, J. & Priestley, P. (1985) Offending Behaviour: Skills & Strategems for Going Straight Batsford
Merrington, S. (1998) A Guide to Setting Up and Evaluating Programmes for Young Offenders ISTD Press
Morrison, B. (1998) As If Granta
Priestley, P. (1999) Victorian Prison Lives: English Prison Biography 1830-1914 Pimlico
Scraton, P. Sim, J. & Skidmore, P. (1991) Prisons Under Protest Open University Press
Stern, V. (1987) Bricks of Shame London: Penguin
Stern, V. (1998) A Sin Against the Future: Imprisonment and the World London: Penguin
Walker, N. (1991) Why Punish? Oxford University Press
Whitfield, D. (ed) (1991) The State of the Prisons London: Routledge

Women and Imprisonment

Carlen, P. (ed) (1985) Criminal Women Polity Press
Kennedy, H. Eve Was Framed
Lamb, W. & the Women of York Correctional (2003) Couldn't Keep it to Myself ReganBooks
Padel, U. & Stevenson, P. (1988) Insiders: Women's Experience of Prison Virago
Worrall, A. (1990) Offending Women London: Routledge

Biography/Autobiography

Boyle, J. (1977) A Sense of Freedom London: Penguin
Krishnamma, S.R. (1992) The Ballad of Lazy l.

Leech, M. (1992) A Product of the System Gollancz
Wilde, O. The Ballad of Reading Gaol

Therapy
Carrell & Laing (1992) The Special Unit, Barlinnee Prison: Its Evolution Through its Art Third Eye
Cox, M. (ed) (1992) Shakespeare Comes to Broadmoor London: Jessica Kingsley Publishers
Jennings & Minde (1992) Art therapy and Dramatherapy: Masks of the Soul London: Jessica Kingsley Publishers
Jones, P. (1996) Drama as Therapy: Theatre as Living London: Routledge
Karp & Holmes (ed) (1991) Psychodrama: Inspiration and Technique London: Routledge
Landy, R. (1993) Persona & Performance London: Jessica Kingsley Publishers
Liebmann, M. (1996) Arts Approaches to Conflict London: Jessica Kingsley Publishers
Moore, P. (1997) Therapy for Groups Arena
Rose, S. (1998) Group Therapy with Troubled Youth London: Sage Publications

Documentaries
Rogerson, H . & Spitzmiller, J. (2006) Shakespeare Behind Bars Philomath Films
Additional Links collected by myself:

Further Links that I came across during my research:

Theatre and Arts in Prison
Krista Brune Report
http://www.communityarts.net/readingroom/archivefiles/2007/01/creating_behind.php
Pan Project
http://www.panproject.org/index.php?option=com_frontpage&Itemid=1
Escape Artists http://www.escapeartists.co.uk/
Gefängnistheater http://www.gefaengnistheater.de/

Prison Critique
Speak Out! On Angela Davis
http://speakoutnow.live.radicaldesigns.org/userdata_display.php?modin=50&uid=46
Speak Out! Links and Ressources

http://speakoutnow.live.radicaldesigns.org/article.php?list=type&type=6
http://socialjustice.ccnmtl.columbia.edu/index.php/Abolish_Prisons

Alternatives to Punishment
http://www.restorativejustice.org/
http://www.toa-servicebuero.de/

Biography of Michael Balfour
Michael Balfour is Chair, Applied Theatre, in the School of Education and Professional Studies, Griffith University, Brisbane, Australia. His research concentrates on theatre in communities, social institutions, and areas of disadvantage and conflict. He is currently co-director of a major Arts and Humanities Research Council (UK) research project, In Place of War (www.inplaceofwar.net), exploring the relationship between performance and war. He is developing work in the area of performance and trauma, in relation to refugees and war veterans. He has worked extensively in prisons in UK and Europe, developing a range of cultural programmes exploring issues of social justice, violence and offending behaviour.

Masters of Peace

edited by Prof. Dr. Wolfgang Dietrich (UNESCO Chair for Peace Studies)

Samrat Schmiem Kumar
Bhakti – the yoga of love
Trans-rational approaches to Peace Studies
Transrational Peaces is a new approach in contemporary Peace Research. It considers the rational and the spiritual sphere of human perception to be essential for the understanding of peace. In this book the Austrian-Indian researcher Samrat Schmiem Kumar presents the Indian tradition of Bhakti Yoga, and demonstrates the value of Indian philosophy for contemporary discussions on peace. In the philosophy of Bhakti, life is a playful and aesthetic relationship between human and the cosmos. The book opens the field of Peace Studies beyond the well-known horizons of the discipline in Europe and the United States.
Bd. 1, 2010, 168 S., 19,90 €, br., ISBN 978-3-643-50130-1

LIT Verlag Berlin – Münster – Wien – Zürich – London
Auslieferung Deutschland / Österreich / Schweiz: siehe Impressumsseite